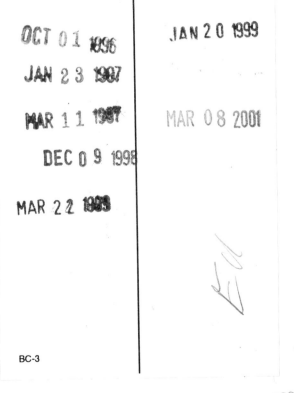

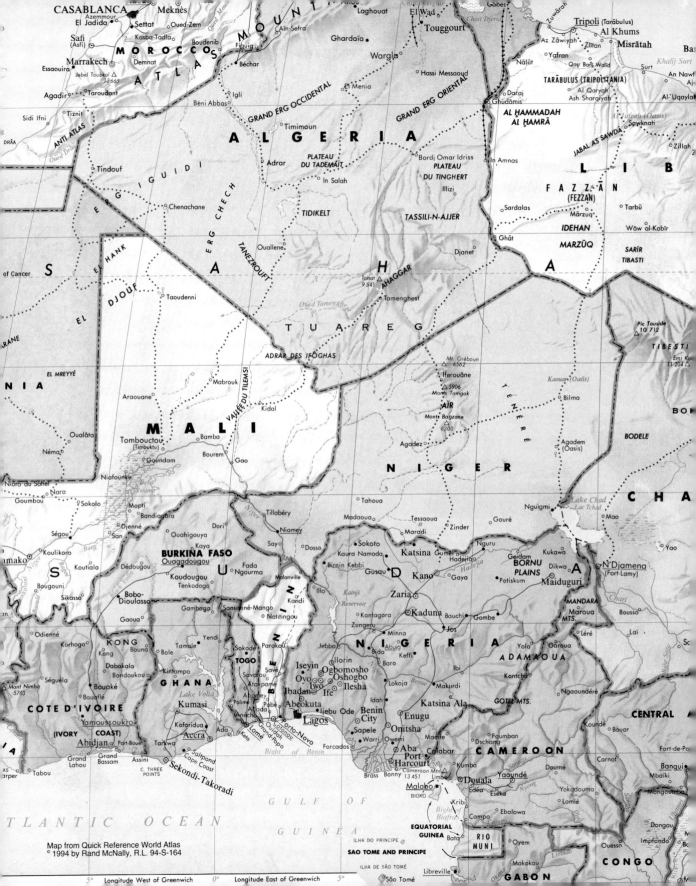

Enchantment of the World

NIGERIA

by Dorothy B. Sutherland

Consultant for Nigeria: Ikem Okoye, Ph.D., Assistant Professor, Art History, Northwestern University, Evanston, Illinois

Consultant for Reading: Robert L. Hillerich, Ph.D., Professor Emeritus, Bowling Green State University; Consultant, Pinellas County Schools, Florida

CHILDRENS PRESS ®
CHICAGO

Nigerian men in traditional embroidered robes

Project Editor: Mary Reidy
Design: Margrit Fiddle
Photo Research: Feldman & Associates, Inc.

Library of Congress Cataloging-in-Publication Data

Sutherland, Dorothy B.
  Nigeria / by Dorothy B. Sutherland.
    p.   cm. – (Enchantment of the world)
  Includes index.
  Summary: Discusses the geography, history, people,
economy, and customs of this West African country–
Africa's most populous nation.
  ISBN 0-516-02634-8
  1. Nigeria–Juvenile literature. [1. Nigeria.]
I. Title. II. Series.
DT515.22.S88 1995   94-24522
966.9–dc20   CIP
                                                  AC

Picture Acknowledgments
AP/Wide World Photos: 50, (3 photos), 52 (2 photos), 53
(left & right), 75 (right), 103
The Bettmann Archive: 39, 40 (2 photos)
© **Lee Boltin:** 36, 76, 79 (2 photos), 82

© **Victor Englebert:** 19
H. Armstrong Roberts: © C. C. Philipp, 14
Impact Visuals: © Sean Sprague, 6, 12, 64, 106, 107; © Scott
Stearns, 8; © Bruce Paton, 29 (bottom), 81, 96 (right)
Lauré Communications: © Jason Lauré, 21, 63, 65 (2
photos), 66, 70 (2 photos), 73, 88 (inset), 99 (2 photos)
North Wind Picture Archives: 38
Odyssey/Frerck/Chicago: © Robert Frerck, Cover bottom
inset, 20 (left), 23, 78 (left), 83, 97 (left), 98
Photri: Cover top inset, 5, 13, 15, 17 (2 photos), 20 (right),
24, 26 (2 photos), 27 (2 photos), 29 (top & top inset), 30
(left), 32, 42, 57, 58 (bottom), 61, 72 (right), 80 (center), 84,
85 (2 photos), 86, 88, 89 (3 photos), 90, 91 (left), 92, 93
(left), 94, 95, 97 (right), 105, 109
Reuters/Bettmann: 75 (left), 101
Root Resources: © Lois Coren, 72 (left), 90 (inset), 93
(right)
SuperStock International, Inc: © Schuster, Cover
Tony Stone Images: © Lawrence Manning, 3, 18, 58 (top);
© Mike Wells, 57
UPI/Bettmann: 35, 45, 47, 48 (2 photos), 49, 53 (center), 55
Valan: © Val & Alan Wilkinson, 30 (right), 31 (2 photos),
68 (2 photos), 78 (right & inset), 80 (left & right), 91
(right), 96 (left & center)
Len W. Meents: Maps on 87, 95, 97, 98
**Courtesy Flag Research Center, Winchester,
Massachusetts 01890:** Flag on back cover
Cover: Woman from Manbila
Cover top inset: Aerial view of Port Harcourt
Cover bottom inset: Carved façade of building in the old
city of Kano

Vendors at the market combine traditional and contemporary clothing.

TABLE OF CONTENTS

Rural Nigerian children at home

Chapter 1

LAND OF DIFFERENCES

Nigeria, we hail thee
Our own dear native land.
Though tribe and tongue may differ
In brotherhood we stand.
Nigerians all are proud to serve
Our sovereign motherland.

This was a song written to celebrate Nigeria's full independence from British rule on October 1, 1960. For a time this song was the national anthem. Although it never became popular, it helps explain a lot about this fascinating country. The line to remember is the third one. The Federal Republic of Nigeria, the official name of the country, has around three hundred "tribes" (ethnic groups), many divided into subgroups. The number of "tongues" (languages and dialects) has been estimated as between three hundred and four hundred.

In addition to "tribes" and "tongues," there are different religions; and, as in the United States, there is separation of church and state with no official state religion. Almost half of Nigerians are Muslims, but not all follow the strictest teachings of their religion. Many of the faithful, in places such as Iran, might find little in common with some Nigerian Muslims.

Choir members outside a Baptist church in Lagos chat with each other before services.

Approximately one-third of the people are Christians of various sects. A small number of Nigerians still cling to ancient beliefs in good and evil spirits. (In fact, even those who are Muslims or Christians do not entirely reject the spirit world of their ancestors.)

Along with this assortment of ethnic groups, languages, and beliefs, there are also vast differences in ways of living. Nigerians may occupy modern apartments in cities or traditional clay houses in villages. They may work as professionals—teachers, doctors, lawyers—or farm according to age-old methods. They may work in the civil service and industry or wander from place to place tending cattle. They may dress in stylish Western clothes, flowing robes, or the strips of leather and feather ornaments of ancient custom.

The reason for this great diversity in Nigerian life is that the country did not develop within natural boundaries as many countries did. It came into being as a result of British colonial rule. The British ruled the territory as part of their empire in the late nineteenth century. They did not settle there in large numbers but ran the country through local chiefs, thus allowing regional differences to remain.

The struggle between traditional ways of doing things and the influence of the West adds to the mixture. This can be seen, for instance, in the contrast between simple villages and nearby modern highways on which high-speed cars hurtle past. When cars on the superhighway between the two major cities of Lagos and Ibadan have to slow down at cloverleaf intersections, women from such villages gather, with their babies on their backs and naked children playing at their feet, to sell such things as yams and goat meat to the temporarily slowed-down motorists.

With all these differences, can there be such a person as a typical Nigerian? You wouldn't think there could be. Travelers to Nigeria, however, remark on a certain independent outlook on life, a self-confidence, and a spirit of enterprise that seem common to Nigerians. Westerners attempting to run businesses in Nigeria praise their employees for their intelligence and energy, but often complain that they do not make good "company men" because they all really have their hearts set on setting up their own businesses.

The spirit of enterprise can be seen in the many Nigerians who go abroad to work and study. It is possible to come across a

Nigerian cabdriver in a big American city who, besides driving a taxi, is studying economics at a local university and playing guitar in a rock band in his spare time. He may well have lived in Paris, London, or both before coming to America.

ONE IN FIVE AFRICANS?

Just how many of these enterprising people are there? Although Nigeria is not the largest country in Africa, it has the largest population. When it comes to finding out just how large the population is, we run into problems. There have been various attempts to take a census of Nigerians, but all have proved difficult. For one thing, people move around a lot; for another, many are very suspicious of census takers. Why are they trying to count heads? Is it a plot to collect more taxes? Is the government trying to interfere with people's religion or way of life? Has it something to do with politics? These sorts of questions worry some people and cause them to give false information, according to what they think will be to their advantage.

In 1980 estimates of the number of Nigerians ran from 77 million to more than 100 million. In 1992 the government made a special effort to take an accurate census. The borders were closed for three days; shops and factories were shut; people were ordered to stay home. In March 1993 it was announced that the result was 88.5 million. There was an immediate outcry. Most people felt this was too low and that 100 million was nearer the mark. There were loud complaints from people who stayed home and never saw a census taker.

So we would seem to be no wiser. It *is* known, however, that of all the people in Africa, at least one in five is Nigerian. Some say it's one in four!

Chapter 2

DIFFERENT "TRIBES," TONGUES, AND RELIGIONS

"It is estimated" is a safe thing to say about any attempt to arrive at numbers of things in Nigeria. That is why we say that there are "around" three hundred ethnic groups in the country. The exact number is unclear because in counting, some people include smaller groups within a larger one and some count each subgroup separately. When the latter way of counting is used, the number can be as high as four hundred. The variety of groups is higher in Nigeria than in any other African country. (That's one thing you can be sure of: whatever is being talked about, Nigeria almost always has more of it. That's why it is often called "the Giant of Africa.")

There are, however, only three major groups in the country, and around 60 percent of Nigerians belong to them.

HAUSA

The Hausa are dominant in the north. They are Muslims who follow the Islam religion and are mainly farmers, traders, and

A Hausa man

merchants. Although farming is the principal occupation, there are also well-developed urban centers. The Hausa have strong political, religious, and cultural institutions.

One very large and important subgroup of the Hausa is the Hausa-Fulani. The Fulani were an ancient ruling class established in small kingdoms, or *emirates*.

In the nineteenth century, the Fulani overran almost all the lands of the Hausa in a *jihad*, or holy war, to reform abuses by those in power. Throughout the country, the Fulani held the important positions in government and were famous for Islamic scholarship.

An Englishman who was once lieutenant-governor of the Northern Nigerian Province wrote of them: "The pure-blooded Fulani is an extremely reserved person. . . . Any manifestation of feeling, such as smiling or laughing, or showing great interest or sorrow or joy, is considered bad form amongst them." (Strangely

A Fulani bridal couple

enough, many people have said the same thing about upper-class English people, who are supposed to keep a "stiff upper lip" in all circumstances.)

The Fulani still consider themselves the aristocrats of the Hausa, even though they do not all live in the same way. Many are "bush" or "cow" Fulani, who live as nomads, tending their own or other people's cattle and never settling in one place.

Personal importance among the Hausa and Hausa-Fulani used to derive from descent from the old rulers of the emirates and from scholarship. In recent times, the country's economic needs have made nonreligious education more valued than Islamic learning, and the status of businessmen and merchants has risen.

YORUBA

The Yoruba are the main people in western Nigeria, and theirs is the biggest city, Lagos, which is a state in itself. It is the largest

*A Yoruba elder dressed
for a council meeting*

city in all of black Africa. The Yoruba are mostly Christian. This particular group came to be called the Yoruba only in the mid-nineteenth century. The Yoruba originally inhabited small, separate kingdoms.

The Yoruba in the southwest were among the first in the country to have Christianity established in their territory. Because of mission schools, they were better educated at an earlier stage and better able to cope with the changes brought by contact with the outside world.

Many of Nigeria's admired writers are Yoruba, and the group is also famous for its marvelous artists.

IGBO

The third largest group is the Igbo, sometimes spelled *Ibo*, who are mostly to be found in the southeast. Igbo life originally centered around small villages, and no great towns were

An Igbo woman

established. The Igbo did not have powerful kings or chiefs until the British appointed some in the colonial period. You might say that seeds of democracy were flourishing hundreds of years ago among these people, who did not believe in letting any of their number get too powerful.

Although most early Igbo were small farmers, many also became skilled craftsmen. When mission schools were set up, the Igbo took advantage of the opportunities that education offered. With their newfound knowledge and their old-time skills, they ventured forth throughout the land, taking many skilled jobs and civil service posts. The first governor-general of independent Nigeria, later its first president, was Dr. Nnamdi Azikiwe, a member of the Igbo group.

The Igbo have a reputation for being exceptionally enterprising and independent. In the late 1960s they attempted to set up a separate state, Biafra, which led to a tragic war. The Igbo have produced many admired artists, sculptors, and writers.

THE KANURI AND THE TIV

Among the host of other groups, two are worth special mention. The Kanuri, most of whom live near Lake Chad in the northeast, are not a large segment of the population, perhaps no more than 4 or 5 percent, but they have a very strong sense of their own identity. They trace their ancestry back a thousand years and are very proud of the fact that when the Fulani were overrunning Hausaland in the nineteenth century, they were not able to conquer Bornu where the Kanuri lived.

The Tiv, in the central part of Benue, also take pride in their uniqueness. They call their part of the country Tivland. The Tiv were never ruled by any kings or chiefs, but ran their lives in small units guided by village elders. They are famous for their traditional theater, song, and dance. In contrast to this creative talent, they make up between one-quarter and one-third of the national army, though they are only 2 percent of the population.

A TANGLE OF TONGUES

With several hundred languages and dialects, how do Nigerians communicate with one another? Because of the British influence, from trading to mission schools to colonization, English is the most widely used language. All official business is conducted in English. There are English-language newspapers, radio, and television programs. All educated Nigerians speak English perfectly, and many novelists, poets, and playwrights use it, or write in their native language and do their own translation into English.

Hausa is the second most common language. (Many people

Kanuri girls (left) and a Tiv chief (right)

who are counted as Hausa are really only speakers of the language, another of the difficulties that arise when trying to gather facts about Nigeria.) Large numbers speak Yoruba and Igbo; then come all the rest.

When those with little or no formal education try to communicate with others, they use something called Nigerian-Pidgin. They use a few English words and versions of English words in a way that follows the pattern of their own language.

Many Nigerians would like to have an official language other than English, which they resent as a reminder that they were once ruled by a foreign power. When the writer Wole Soyinka was awarded the Nobel Prize for Literature in 1986, they protested that he should not have accepted it because it is a European prize and he wrote in English.

Of course, how would they ever choose which language to use? It is unlikely that the Igbo or Yoruba would consent to give way

17

Muslims praying outdoors

to Hausa or that the Hausa would let another tongue come out on top. It is likely that English will remain, particularly because Nigerians who have mastered it are able to travel, work, and study in any English-speaking country they choose. Nowadays, many children, especially in the cities such as Lagos, speak only English and don't bother to learn the language of their ancestors.

ISLAM

The religion that holds Allah to be the one true God is called Islam and its followers are called Muslims. This is the religion practiced by almost half of Nigeria's population, and its particular stronghold is in the north among the Hausa and Hausa-Fulani. The form most followed is Sunni, which is practiced by more than 80 percent of all Muslims throughout the world.

Sunni Islam calls for belief in both Allah and in his prophet Muhammad. It demands that Muslims pray five times each day,

*A young man
transcribes pages
of the Koran,
the Muslim holy book.*

give alms to the poor, observe the special time of year known as
Ramadan, and make a pilgrimage (*hajj*) to the Holy City of Mecca
in Saudi Arabia. It is not easy for all Nigerian Muslims to fulfill
all these requirements. Working farmers and cattle herders, for
instance, find it difficult to fast during the day at Ramadan as
they should and still have enough energy for their hard physical
work. Many cannot afford to go to Mecca, but those who do gain
great prestige.

The most important people among the Nigerian Sunni are the
mallamai, who are either scholars in Islamic law, often advising
local officials, or teachers who instruct at all levels of religious
education. The teachers are often called on to take part in

The muezzin *(left) calls Muslims to prayer
from the minaret of the mosque (right).*

ceremonies that are not Muslim. They are asked to participate to
give the occasion an extra touch of class.

Although Muslims are supposed to worship Allah as the one
true God, many Nigerians play it extra safe by calling on spirits
to help at times of illness or other misfortunes. They may wear
amulets inscribed with quotations from the Koran, the Muslim
holy book, to ward off evil. The spirit cult, *Bori,* is chiefly
followed by those the Hausa consider to be on a lower social
scale. In this they include women, hunters, butchers, and
blacksmiths.

Churchgoers carry their prié-dieux, *"kneelers," to services.*

CHRISTIANITY

Christianity was introduced by the missionaries who came from Portugal in the sixteenth and seventeenth centuries and from Great Britain in the eighteenth and nineteenth centuries. It was established in the regions where the Muslims did not already hold sway, that is, the lands mainly populated by the Igbo and the Yoruba. The missionaries started schools as well as churches, and those Nigerians who grasped the chance to get themselves educated had to study the Bible along with other subjects.

Of course, the forms of Christianity taught varied because the missionaries came from different churches. In Nigeria there are Anglicans, Roman Catholics, Presbyterians, Methodists, and Lutherans. Others have joined such groups as the Salvation Army and the Jehovah's Witnesses.

In the late nineteenth century, some Nigerians threw off the domination of the mission churches and set up their own African, often called Ethiopian, churches, which were run by Nigerian ministers and members of their congregations. These people did not want to reject Christianity, they simply wanted to run their own churches without foreign interference. In the twentieth century, even the mission churches came to be run by the Nigerians themselves.

Other Christian churches have emerged and have grown greatly since 1945. These are the *Aladura*, "prayer," churches. They developed because some people thought that the other Christian churches were too much concerned with people getting to Heaven and not enough with helping the individual to deal with problems here on earth. These Aladura churches often promote faith healing or pay attention to the meaning of dreams and visions. Some have very boisterous services with singing and dancing. Some even allow old customs such as a man or woman having more than one wife or husband at the same time.

TRADITIONAL RELIGION

In remote rural areas ancient forms of religion still exist. Local spirits are worshiped. These are usually connected with natural features such as rivers or forests. The help of these spirits is sought in producing good harvests or success in trading. Sometimes the help of ancestors also is called on.

There is strong belief in the evil powers of witches and sorcerers and not much trust in such things as modern medicine. As has been said before, many Nigerian Christians and Muslims do not forget the old spirit religion. Wole Soyinka, in his book about his boyhood, *Aké*, describes his mother—a church member—

A priest-chief at a traditional religious shrine

spinning tales to her children about her brother's adventures as a tree demon, an *oro*. Aké's mother's nickname was "the Wild Christian." Near the city of Ibadan is a shrine to the river goddess, Oshun. In a grove, surrounded by strange and beautiful carved figures, visitors still come to ask Oshun's blessing and to have a priestess pour water from the sacred river over their heads.

When African slaves arrived in areas in the Caribbean and South America where the Roman Catholic Church was established, the priests set about converting them. Many who learned about the various saints blended their ideas about the saints with their memories of the good and evil spirits of their old religion. This gave rise to special forms of religion that still exist today in places such as Brazil, the Caribbean islands, and parts of the United States. *Voodoo*, for instance, derives from such a mixture of Christianity and ancient African religions, most especially a religion known as *vodun*, which once was practiced in the ancient West African kingdom of Dahomey.

Villages in central Nigeria

Chapter 3

THE LIE OF THE LAND AND ITS CLIMATE

The continent of Africa starts out wide at the top and then the west coast takes a right-angle bend to the east, then another huge bend to the south. Nigeria, in West Africa, lies at that inner bend. It covers an area of 356,669 square miles (923,768 square kilometers) and is in the part of Africa known as sub-Saharan; that is, lying to the south of the great Sahara desert. It is in the tropical zone, not far north of the equator, the hottest region of the world.

In the south Nigeria's coastline stretches 478 miles (769 kilometers) along the Gulf of Guinea and the Bight (bay) of Benin, which open into the mid-Atlantic Ocean. To the west of Nigeria is the country of Benin, to the east is Cameroon, and to the north is Niger. (Because one of Nigeria's states is called Niger, this can cause confusion.)

When Nigeria became a British colony in 1900, it was divided into just two sections: Northern and Southern. When it became the independent Federal Republic of Nigeria in 1960, there were three regions, called states. By the late 1970s there were twelve states. Then the number increased to nineteen, and by the early 1990s there were thirty. It may not be safe to stop counting yet.

Left: The Niger and Benue Rivers meet and form a lake.
Right: The mountainous eastern border with Cameroon

THE LAND

Because tourism as a business has only recently begun to interest Nigerians, many of the country's scenic beauties are unknown to outsiders. There are spectacular views in the mountainous eastern border with Cameroon, but this region is so difficult to reach that only an adventurous few make the trek. Guidebooks to West Africa often say that the Nigerian people are more interesting than most of the scenery.

Prepare yourself for yet another Niger! This time it's a river. The Niger River—its name means "river of rivers"—is some 2,600 miles (about 4,184 kilometers) long, with only about one-third of its course actually in Nigeria. It rises in the country of Guinea, northwest of Nigeria, flows first in a northeast direction into the country of Mali, then southeastward, passing through the west of the country of Niger. It finally enters Nigeria at a place called

A train passes through savanna land (left). Fulani travel on foot with their cattle (right).

Gaya in the northwest, and continues southeast to the central plateau region where its main tributary, the Benue River, comes in from the east to join it to form a lake area 2 miles (3 kilometers) wide. The Niger then flows directly south until it splits into a series of rivers that make up the huge delta area. This area forms a triangle 150 miles (241 kilometers) from top to bottom and 200 miles (322 kilometers) wide at the coast where all the rivers flow into the Gulf of Guinea.

Just as nothing else in Nigeria is uniform, the land also is greatly varied. The north is flat, an area of savanna, coarse tropical grass, with sparse, stunted trees. This is an area where Fulani cattle herds wander the land. The largest cattle market in the country is to be found near the city of Kano. Many Hausa are settled here on small farms, most producing only enough of such crops as yams and millet to sustain their own communities.

In the extreme northeast corner of Nigeria, the country forms part of the shore of a most extraordinary lake. This is Lake Chad, but you might think a better name for it would be the Incredible Shrinking Lake. In February, the area covered by water may be as great as 9,995 square miles (25,887 square kilometers). In July, the water may cover only 3,800 square miles (9,842 square kilometers). This strange lake is one of the world's largest sources of freshwater fish.

The middle region of Nigeria is the least populated area, much of it still savanna. The central Jos Plateau, however, 3,937 feet (1,200 meters) above sea level, has the coolest temperature in the country and the most pleasant views, with green grass and rolling hills. Interesting trees grow here, such as the baobab, which produces gourdlike fruit, and the tamarind, which bears seeds used to flavor food and drinks. The area around the town of Jos is noted for its tin mines.

Much of the north and central part consists of *bush*, land covered with mixed vegetation. The Fulani who tend cattle here are called "Bush Fulani."

The southern region has the most people and the most industry. In the west of its coastal area is the huge city-state of Lagos. The second-largest city in the country, Ibadan, is also in this southern region. The greatest sources of Nigeria's riches are here—oil, natural gas, and valuable trees. Sadly, the magnificent forests that once were here have been severely reduced, and many great trees such as the mahogany have given way to oil palm trees from which the growers can make more money. The delta area still claims to be the "plywood capital of the world."

The coastal region is one of lagoons and swamps overgrown with tangled, low-growing mangrove trees. The mouths of the several rivers of the delta area are clogged with sandbars.

Some views of the land
include Lake Chad
(top inset), green grass
of the Jos Plateau (center),
and a logging area in
the rain forest (bottom inset).

Airplanes (left) can take travelers to most sections of the country and taxis (right) can be hired, but a price must be agreed on first.

There are many ways to get from one region to another. A government airline, Nigerian Airways, flies to all the major cities, with connections to remote parts of the interior. There are also many smaller private airlines, such as Kabo Air, Zenith Air, Hold Trade Air, Trans-Sahel Airlines, and Okada Air. It is also possible to travel around much of the country by railway, but the trains are usually very slow. Minibuses, on the other hand, go at reckless—and illegal—speeds of 87 miles (140 kilometers) per hour. They are very crowded but are cheaper and faster than bigger buses. Then there are taxis for hire that will travel long distances, but fares must be carefully haggled over before setting out. Anyone wanting to go to a really remote spot will have to walk the last part of the way. Many places are also reachable by the plentiful rivers and streams.

THE CLIMATE

The climate, of course, varies widely. In the north, there is one long rainy season from May to mid-September. Then comes the

Left: Although frequently overcrowded, river ferries are a pleasant way to travel.
Right: When the harmattan *is blowing, it is difficult to see.*

harmattan—a dry, hot wind blowing down from the Sahara. Novelist Chinua Achebe has one of his characters describe being in the harmattan at midday as like sitting with a hair dryer blowing full in one's face. The anthropologist Laura Bohannan describes the experience as living in "an aquarium of dust through which we saw the sky grey or primrose, but never blue." This terrible wind, so hot during the day, can also be nastily chilly at night. It does not stop short at the boundaries of the northern region, but that is where it is at its worst. Water shortages are often severe at this time: streams and wells dry up; wooden articles can dry and crack, as can human lips and skin.

In the south, the old saying, "It's not the heat, it's the humidity," is certainly true. Although the temperature in Lagos, for instance, in July or August is about the same or even lower than it is at that time in Washington, D.C., or Tokyo, or Rome, the humidity is almost unbearable. In August there is a lull between two rainy seasons. One lasts from February to July and the other from September to early November.

Chapter 4

NIGERIA BEFORE
IT WAS NIGERIA

IN THE MISTS OF TIME

To learn about the history of the area we now know as Nigeria, we have to go back many centuries, before there was any such country. All countries have a past for which there is no written record, and much of our knowledge has to be worked out from studying ancient objects found in places where people once lived. In Nigeria's case there are many more years about which we know little or nothing than there are years of records.

Until recently, the outside world assumed that ancient Africa south of the Sahara had existed in an uncivilized state of chaos, not worth any serious study. In the 1930s, however, a colonial tin-mining operation in central Nigeria dug up a treasure trove of terra-cotta figurines and portrait heads and other evidence that there had been an ancient society of great achievement there. Carbon-14 dating—the modern technique that can determine age by measuring the radioactivity of minerals found in certain materials—placed the existence of this society between approximately 900 B.C. and A.D. 500. This society is now known as

Opposite page: Waterfall near Ilorin

the Nok Culture, named after the village in which the treasures were unearthed. Some of the figurines and heads are two thousand years old and as advanced in artistic skill as the ancient Greek sculptures. It is thought that the ability of these people to cast iron developed around 500 B.C.—before the skill was known in ancient Egypt.

In recent decades, the search for the origins of human development has led many scientists to Africa. The famous paleontologist, Louis Leakey, wrote in the 1960s that it was "the African continent which saw the emergence of the basic stock which eventually gave rise to . . . man as we know him today." His conclusion is right in line with the Yoruba legend that Ife, in south Nigeria, home of their founder, Oranmiyan, was the spot where God first created humankind.

It has been pointed out that regardless of where the main groups that migrated to Nigeria originated, they probably intermarried with people already living in the regions where they settled. Migrations across vast areas probably would have been made mainly by men because of the hardships of the journey. Therefore, they had to find wives in already established communities. The societies and customs encountered by the first European travelers to venture into Nigeria probably evolved from a mixture of peoples who were originally quite different.

Now that the study of Africa's past has come to interest more and more scholars, archaeologists who study objects, and anthropologists who study people, are not the only people searching for evidence of how the various groups developed. Linguists, who study language, are hopeful that by finding the roots of the many "tongues," they may clear more mist from the past.

By the sixteenth century Kano was known as a center for trading and Islamic study. This photograph was taken in 1920.

GLIMMERS OF LIGHT

The outside world began to learn about the Nigerian area with the growth of trade. North Africa wanted gold and ivory; sub-Saharan Africa needed salt. Those who controlled these things became powerful, and before the year 1000, the empire of Kanen-Bornue in the northeast had grown rich by trading. Through trading connections with the Arab world the people of this region became converted to Islam.

The original Hausa people had settled in the northern part of Nigeria, but no one knows quite when. By the thirteenth century there were many well-established states. Each one was named for the city at its center. Each city was surrounded by farms, enclosed by mud walls, and ringed by deep, wide ditches. In times of warfare people from the nearby countryside could find refuge within the walls. And warfare was a fairly constant fact of life, for although these states could sometimes cooperate when threatened by a common enemy, they all too often fought among themselves. The chief source of rivalry was trade, and war or no war, the Hausa never abandoned trading. Each state had a king and was ruled by Islamic law. Among these city-states, Kano was the

An ivory saltcellar, made in Nigeria, is more than 1 foot (0.3 meter) high.

greatest. By the sixteenth century, it was famous as a center not only of trade but of Muslim learning.

In the southwest the focus of trade and of fine sculpture became Benin City, inhabited by the Edo, or Bini. (Another possible confusion here: Benin City is *not* in the country of Benin, which is next door to Nigeria.) Benin City was a centrally important religious city ruled by a powerful king and priests whose gods demanded human sacrifices for their ceremonies. These rulers were feared for their almost absolute power over their own and neighboring people.

Early European traders were able to reach this city by sailing to the Bight of Benin and then navigating up the Benin River in small craft. Successive kings of the city seized on the chance to enrich themselves through the new commerce. The sculptors made many fine objects such as saltcellars for sale to the traders.

THE AGE OF DISCOVERY

In the late fourteenth century, Abraham Cresques of the Spanish island of Majorca made the first map of West Africa. Although it was far from accurate, the fact that it was produced at all shows that European interest in the area had been stirred. Those who traded with North African countries had learned from them of possible riches to be found farther south.

The world was entering what came to be known as the Age of Discovery. Seafaring people—Portuguese, Spanish, Venetians, Dutch, English—set sail in search of new lands and new wealth. Columbus was not the only one who sought a new route to India. The era could perhaps be compared to the twentieth-century Space Age.

The early sailors were just as daring as the astronauts. They were completely cut off when they left harbor—no friendly voices from the land guided them. Regions such as West Africa were not simply unexplored, they were often believed to be inhabited by evil spirits and other dangers. "Here be monsters" old mapmakers used to put on their charts when they ran out of real information.

In reality in West Africa it wasn't monsters that had to be feared. The real dangers were the tiny disease-carrying creatures such as mosquitoes and tsetse flies. Before there were medicines to treat malaria, the delta area of Nigeria was so dangerous for Europeans that there was a saying:

"Beware, beware, the Bight of Benin
Where few come out, though many go in."

The first traders to reach Benin City in 1474 were Portuguese who had set out with the backing of their prince, known as

Henry the Navigator

Henry the Navigator. Others soon followed. Merchants went in search of gold and missionaries in search of souls to save. By the end of the fifteenth century the merchants were doing brisk trade in ivory and pepper, and the pope had issued a decree, a Papal Bull, declaring that most of Africa was to belong to Portugal. The rulers of Benin City had allowed some Portuguese to settle in the city. One or two of the kings even learned to speak Portuguese, and traces of that language were still to be found there in the late eighteenth century. But the churches and monasteries that were set up were no match for the well-established local religion, and attempts to win converts were abandoned.

By the mid-1550s, the Protestant Reformation, rejecting the Catholic Church, had taken place in Europe, and many countries no longer bowed to the pope's authority. His decree that most of Africa belonged to Portugal was ignored; only Spain continued to obey it. The English embarked on a very long association with what was to become Nigeria.

Their first expedition to Benin City, in 1553, was hardly a success; 140 men set out but only 40 reached home again.

People were lined up, yoked, and marched long distances to be sold into slavery.

(Remember that rhyme about the Bight of Benin?) Some thirty years later, two ships commanded by a Captain Welsh were able to get to Benin City and back with a cargo that Welsh described as "Elephants' teeth, oyle of palm, cloth made of Cotton wool very curiously woven, and cloth made of the barke of palm trees [All his spelling]." The "oyle of palm" was to become one of Nigeria's chief and most enduring exports, and the rivers in the area where it is still plentiful are called the Oil Rivers.

THE EVIL TRADE

Sad to say, oil, cloth, pepper, ivory—even gold—were not the only source of wealth to be developed. With the discovery of the New World of America and the West Indies, a demand arose for slaves to work in the new mines and plantations established there.

In Africa the idea of slavery was not new. Age-old and unceasing tribal war had caused countless defeated people to be enslaved by their conquerors. When the call for slaves came from across the Atlantic, rivals were perfectly willing to sell off captive

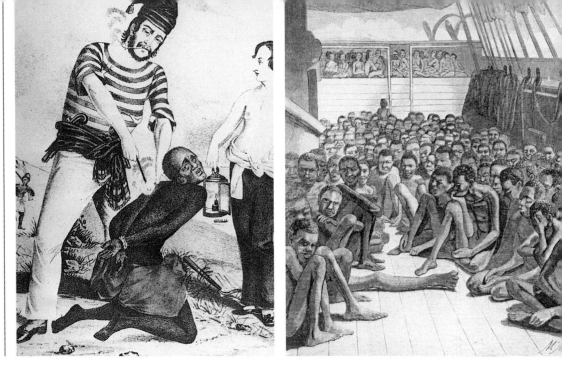

Slaves were branded (right) and crowded onto the decks of ships (far right) for transport.

human beings as if they were any other form of trade goods.

For the first fifty years of this loathsome trade, the Portuguese had the monopoly because of that papal decree. When other nations joined in the hunt for Africa's riches, they were just as eager to trade in whatever was available, materials or humans. All the countries of West Africa were victims of the slave trade, but it was particularly convenient for slave ships to operate in the many Nigerian River estuaries, where they could find safe harbor while waiting for their human cargo to be brought to them.

To be sure, slavery had existed for centuries in many parts of the world. But what made the African slave trade so exceptionally terrible was the wholesale treatment of people as cattle, the horrible conditions aboard the slave ships. Many writers have told of the cruel treatment in the European forts in which the slaves were first collected and of the dreadful "Middle Passage," the route ships took across the mid-Atlantic.

The impact on Nigeria was corrupting, as greedy chiefs went to greater and greater lengths to keep up with the demand for slaves that made them rich. They often captured the inhabitants of whole villages, not only those of their enemies but those of even their closely related neighbors when the human well seemed to be running dry. Also, in the seventeenth century those who wished to build up their power began to exchange slaves for guns, thus increasing the violence of tribal warfare.

This evil traffic continued through the sixteenth, seventeenth, and eighteenth centuries, with many nations taking part. Not only were the different countries raiding Africa for slaves, they were involved in acts of piracy against one another, leading to complete lawlessness on the seas between West Africa and the West Indies.

At the height of the slave trade England, now joined with Scotland, Ireland, and Wales, as Great Britain had cornered more than half of the market because of its military control of the river estuaries. Then slowly, slowly, as they began to learn of the cruelties of the system from Africans who lived in Europe and from the missionaries and travelers to the region, the British public began to turn against it. At last, in 1808, an Act of Parliament banned slaves from being carried on British ships or landed in any British colonies.

The Danish government was the first, in 1802, to declare the slave trade illegal. In 1808 the United States forbade the importing of any more slaves, although the practice of slavery continued for more than fifty years. Total abolition did not come until 1865, near the end of the Civil War. The slave trade, as we know, had a lasting effect on the course of United States history. In South America, Brazil has a larger black population than any other country except Nigeria, all descended from slaves.

Slavery did not end just because people realized its evils but because, as mills and factories and machinery were introduced, slavery was seen to be inefficient and unprofitable.

Chapter 5

THE COUNTRY

TAKES SHAPE

EXPLORATION AND COLONIZATION

In the late eighteenth century great interest in the geography of sub-Saharan Africa arose in Britain. This was originally a scientific rather than a commercial interest. Societies such as the African Association, founded in 1788, put up money for expeditions to explore hitherto unknown territory. Although the explorations were in the end invaluable for trade, that was not the goal of the many heroic men who first braved dreadful hardships to discover what these unknown lands were really like.

One of the most famous of these men was Mungo Park, a Scottish surgeon, whose ambition was to find the true course of the Niger River. From ancient times the existence of such a great river had been known. Some thought it was a tributary of the Nile, flowing under the desert sands. Some said it flowed to the east, some to the west. It was confused with other rivers, such as the Gambia and the Senegal. In 1796 Mungo Park, after suffering countless dangers and hair-raising escapes, finally was able to record that he saw "the long sought for majestic Niger, glittering in the morning sun, broad as the Thames at Westminster, and flowing gently to *the eastward*." It was many years, however,

Opposite page: The Niger River

before the world knew just where the Niger flowed. In 1805 Park was commissioned by the British government to explore the river. He vowed to find where it flowed out to sea or "perish in the attempt." Perish he did, along with all of his companions, possibly in the river of Bussa, possibly at the hands of hostile people—no one knows exactly how. Park, however, had expected to find the mouth of the Niger much farther south than it really is. It was not until thirty years later, after other disastrous attempts, that the Oil Rivers were discovered to be the delta where the Niger flowed into the Atlantic.

SAVING SOULS

The African Association soon added to its aim of exploration the goal of bringing "Christianity and commerce" to the region. In the nineteenth century missionaries of all varieties of Christianity were unstoppable in their determination to rescue the Africans from what the Christians thought was religious darkness.

Wave after wave came to Nigeria. Interestingly, some of these missionaries were black Christians from Great Britain and Sierra Leone who had themselves been captured as slaves when they were children. No matter how many died of natural causes— malaria, other fevers, or natural disasters—or were killed by hostile groups, others kept on coming. The most important thing the missionaries did was to set up schools. Although these were sometimes criticized for being inefficient and for failing to teach proper discipline, they opened the door to a wider world for Nigerians. The missionaries were left in complete charge of education until the British opened the first nonreligious government school in 1899.

A 1922 photograph shows barrels of palm oil waiting to be loaded for shipment.

CONFLICT AND COMMERCE

The British were determined to stamp out the slave trade. But first they had to convince those engaged in it—the local chiefs who had been doing very well out of selling slaves—that it could be just as profitable to deal in such things as palm oil and ivory. One measure of their success is that in 1806 the amount of palm oil imported into Liverpool, England, was 150 tons (136,080 kilograms); in 1839 it was 13,600 tons (12,337,920 kilograms).

Trading in the Oil Rivers area was, at first, done mainly from ships of rival merchants, manned by very rough characters. The ships' masters were cruel, not only to the Africans with whom they dealt but also to their own crews. The local groups often responded with vicious attacks on the merchants while also fighting one another.

In 1849 the British decided to try to bring some order into the area by appointing a representative of the British government as consul of the Bights of Biafra and Benin. This was the beginning of official British entry into Nigeria. Until then naval vessels had only seized slave ships at sea. Now British forces were on Nigerian land and attempts were made to settle disputes with leaders and make treaties with them. The first major takeover by the British was their occupation in 1851 of Lagos, where rival leaders had been at war.

In 1854 a historic venture took place that was to open up new prospects for commerce. A British merchant ship, the *Pleiad*, sailed up the Niger to Benue and was able to stay there trading for four months. What made this a historic event was that *not a single one of its sixty-six-man crew died*. This was the first time such a thing had happened. It was due to the discovery of quinine as a treatment for malaria.

With this one great danger reduced, trading became better organized, and merchants were able to move farther and farther into the country. The merchants wanted protection from often hostile groups. Many of the native people wanted an authority to see that they were fairly treated by the merchants, and they also needed protection from their enemies, because this was a time of war among the Yoruba and of Fulani conquest of the Hausa lands. The British gradually became more and more involved in "peace-keeping" military actions.

COLONIZATION

The British had no great enthusiasm for this involvement, which was thought to be too expensive. They considered pulling out of all of West Africa except Sierra Leone. By the 1880s, however, they had changed their minds. Many European

The entrance to an Igbo chief's compound, from a 1920 photograph

nations—France, Germany, Belgium, Spain—also thought of the possibility of finding wealth in Africa. So began what the *Times* of London called, in a phrase that became famous, "the scramble for Africa."

In the fifteenth century, the pope had declared that most of Africa "belonged" to Portugal. Four hundred years later, in 1885, the major European nations held a conference in Berlin, Germany, and decided which part of Africa was to "belong" to which country. Nigeria was among the territories allotted to Britain.

By 1900 the British had formed the Protectorate of Northern Nigeria and the Protectorate of Southern Nigeria. In 1914 these were merged as the Colony and Protectorate of Nigeria. The top British official was known as the governor-general.

The first and most famous of these, Sir Frederick (later, Lord) Lugard, devised a system of running the country known as "indirect rule," by which the country was administered through local chiefs. This was intended to keep the peace by disturbing the fabric of Nigerian life as little as possible. Trouble arose, however, in parts of the country such as Tivland, where there

47

Early photographs show a woman having her hair dressed (right) and a woman working outside her mat house (far right).

were no chiefs and the British simply appointed some. In one instance in 1929, in the Igbo-speaking region not far from Port Harcourt, there was so much anger at the local chiefs chosen by the British that a most unusual rebellion took place—the "Women's Uprising." The women of the area, fearing more taxation and impatient that their men were doing nothing to resist, took up arms themselves and both police and troops had to be called in to defeat them. Many women were killed or injured, but the rebellion did bring about change in the local government.

The British relied on local rule, of course, largely because there was no great desire among British families to settle in Nigeria with its hot, unhealthy climate. In 1925 there were no more than two hundred British officials running a country of some twenty million people.

STEPS TO FREEDOM

After World War I (1914-1918), the desire for independence took root in Nigeria, as in other European colonies in Africa. In that war Nigerian troops had been used to fight for British interests.

In the 1940s Nigerian leaders met to discuss the country's future.

The thought grew that if ordinary Nigerians were good enough to fight, they should be good enough to have a voice in how they were governed instead of just being represented by *emirs*, or chiefs. This feeling became even stronger after World War II (1939-1945), when Nigerians again were called upon to do battle for their colonial rulers.

Following a period of labor troubles, intergroup strife, and anti-British writings by Nigerian journalists, a central Legislative Council was set up in 1947. In addition, there were three Houses of Assembly—one for the northern region, one for the western region, and one for the eastern region. For the first time, Nigerians other than officials were given a voice. These nonofficials were, however, still appointed. Then in 1951 Nigerians were given the right to vote for their own representatives. But not all Nigerians—just adult male taxpayers. These assemblies still reported to the British government.

In the next few years there was much rearranging of the system and argument about the central government's interference in the regions. Lagos became a separate federal territory in 1954.

There were nationwide celebrations when Nigeria gained independence.
Dr. Nnamdi Azikiwe (bottom right) became the first president.

Chapter 6

INDEPENDENCE

At last, in 1960, Nigeria gained its independence, complete with a Parliament—Senate and House of Representatives—and a prime minister. The members of Parliament were elected by all adult males and females, except in the north, where women were not allowed to vote by Islamic law. At first there was still a British governor-general, but he had no political power and simply acted as a representative of the British queen. In 1961 he departed, and his position was filled, for the first time, by a Nigerian, Dr. Nnamdi Azikiwe. As an important journalist, Azikiwe had been active in the push for independence. In 1963 Nigeria became a republic, and Dr. Azikiwe was its first president. This meant that Queen Elizabeth II was no longer queen of Nigeria, but the country kept its ties to Britain by becoming a member of the Commonwealth of Nations, an association of former colonies of Britain set up to help one another, particularly in matters of trade.

THE WINDING ROAD TO DEMOCRACY

The fourth line of the song quoted at the beginning of this book, "In brotherhood we stand," was wishful thinking. There

Aguiyi-Ironsi (left) became head of state in January 1966 and was followed in July, after his assassination, by Yakubu Gowan (right).

have been many violent quarrels on the road to brotherhood and democracy. Nigeria, however, is determined to get there.

In the first thirty-two years of independence, there were twenty-three years of military government. Although many believe that such governments can rise above regional loyalty to advance national unity, Nigerians do not want their strong men to be tyrants. No military leader is expected to settle in for life. Nigerians believe that no dictator should be allowed to get a grip on the country. Nigeria has had the most outspoken press, radio, and television in all of Africa, and the voices of writers and popular singers are loudly raised against abuses. Although people have been jailed or exiled for criticizing the government, they have not suffered for long without public protest.

Here is how the scene has changed and re-changed since 1960. Independence started with an elected Parliament. A military coup to end government corruption came in January 1966, when Major General Aguiyi-Ironsi became head of state. In July of the same year Aguiyi-Ironsi was assassinated by rival army officers, and General Yakubu Gowon took over. He was overthrown in 1975.

Shehu Shagari (left) was elected president in 1979. However, Muhammad Bahari (center) led a coup and took power in 1983. Then in 1985 Ibrahim Babangida (right) took over.

General Murtala Mohammed came to power, only to be assassinated the next year. Then came General Olusegun Obasanjo, who handed power over to a civilian government in 1979. Shehu Shagari became president, but he was thrown out in 1983 in a coup led by General Muhammad Buhari, himself replaced in 1985 by General Ibrahim Babangida, who promised to restore civilian government by 1992.

Babangida organized an election in 1993 that was won by a civilian chief, M.K.O. Abiola, but the general suspended the election results and refused to let Abiola become president. Confusion loomed, and another army officer, Major General Sani Abacha, seized the presidency in a military coup. Were hopes for democracy crushed? Was Nigeria never to have another civilian president?

Despite the changing governments in Nigeria, many of the traditional religious leaders, such as the *oni*, "king," of Ife and the sultan of Sokoto, remain important. Although they have no official government power, politicians must keep on good terms with them because they have great influence over their followers.

WAR AND OIL

Two major events stand out in the history of Nigeria since independence. The first was a dreadful war that could have permanently destroyed all chance of the country's ever achieving unity. The second was an oil boom that could have made Nigeria a major power. Neither the worst fear nor the highest hope was realized.

BIAFRA

It was not long after independence that the Nigerians became unhappy with their central government. The government was largely controlled by the Hausa-Fulani, which caused resentment among other groups. In January 1966 Igbo officers in the army mutinied and overthrew the civilian government. Major General Aguiyi-Ironsi took control of the country. The Hausa-Fulani resented his government and fighting broke out. Many Igbos were killed, among them Ironsi, and many fled to the eastern section of the country. General Yakubu Gowon became the new military leader of the country.

In May 1967 the Igbo-controlled eastern region declared itself the independent Republic of Biafra. The central government imposed an economic blockade, and then war broke out. As the war grew worse, other African nations—Ethiopia, Ghana, Cameroon, and Niger—tried to intervene to make peace, but the fierce fighting continued. There was much loss of life and property, and reports and pictures of pitiful Biafran women and children refugees stirred worldwide attention but not practical help. The Biafran cause became hopeless and by January 1970 it was all over.

Starving Nigerian children were one tragic result of the Biafran War.

Much credit has been given to General Gowon for the steps he took to heal the country. He declared that no medals were to be given to soldiers on the winning side and that there was to be no killing of those on the losing side. He said the war was to produce "no victors and no vanquished." Many Igbos had their lost property restored, and many returned to former jobs and posts in the Nigerian army. Whereas in other African countries civil wars have dragged on and on, the Biafran War, because of Gowon, did not leave the usual desire for vengeance. Some even say that this taste of civil war acted as an inoculation and Nigerians say "Never again!"

OIL BOOM AND BUST

In the mid-1950s petroleum had been discovered in the coastal area. By the time world oil prices jumped sky-high in the 1970s, Nigeria was one of the world's largest producers of this precious stuff. Nigeria suddenly became rich beyond its dreams and an important player in the world's economic game. Not only did some individuals become millionaires but the government, instead of being short of money, had billions and billions of dollars in spare cash.

Lots of people went a little mad, going on shopping sprees for such things as expensive foreign cars and fancy imported foods. The government went wild, too, with grand building schemes. The new capital was started, along with new universities, superhighways, and television stations.

Unfortunately, the bonanza didn't last. Worldwide recession set in. Countries began to cut back oil imports and oil prices fell. Nigeria found itself in a real economic mess. By the mid-1980s income from oil had fallen to just a fifth of what it had been. Meanwhile, farming had been neglected and Nigeria, which once had exported food, was now importing it. Industries such as car assembly plants had to close down because they couldn't afford to buy parts. Tremendous sums of money had been wasted. Many people, including civilian and military officials at the highest levels, had swindled the government and diverted money into their own pockets. The government's worst mistake had been to waste much of the money on military equipment and on glamorous buildings and roads instead of using it to invest in productive areas such as education, agriculture, and industry.

Babangida put more money into developing agriculture.
Inset: A worker on an oil rig

General Ibrahim Babangida introduced many reforms, cutting back government staffs, putting more money into farming, and banning the import of many luxury items. People who had spent money as if there were no tomorrow found that tomorrow had arrived, and they had to get used to changing their lifestyle. Being ever enterprising, some people who had bought Mercedes or BMW cars in their days of wealth simply turned round and used them as taxicabs when times got hard.

Nigeria is still much worse off than it was in the oil boom days. A few people have managed to stay wealthy, but there is much poverty and unemployment.

Away from the large cities, the people live in small village compounds (above) surrounded by gardens. Their houses are clay, with clay or thatch roofs (below).

Chapter 7

THE WAYS THEY LIVE

COMPOUND LIVING

Until recently, 80 percent of Nigerians lived in rural compounds. Now more and more people live in cities and towns.

A traditional rural compound consists of a number of dwellings occupied by a headman, his immediate family, and assorted other relations. Compounds may be enclosed by walls of matting and sticks or of mud. A group of neighboring compounds makes up a village. The people in the village are usually all related through a common ancestor. Each compound is surrounded by a garden of vegetables, such as corn and yams, tended by the women.

The dwellings in the compound are collections of clay houses for different purposes—cooking, sleeping, and receiving guests. The types of houses vary with the area they are found in, because they are built with local material. In the northernmost, driest areas there are round houses made of clay bricks with flat clay roofs. In the middle section of the country, the clay houses have sloping, thatched grass roofs. In the forest areas, houses may be rectangles with roofs of matting or—for richer people—tin. In the coastal regions, where the soil is too sandy to make clay bricks, the houses are constructed of bamboo, tied together with ropes and matting, with roofs of bamboo leaves. The ropes and matting are made of raffia from the plentiful palm trees.

Such compounds are governed by traditional rules designed to preserve harmony in a situation where life is lived at very close quarters and where everyone knows everyone else's business. There have to be ways of getting along together and of dealing with such natural human feelings as jealousy and anger.

Each village has a chief, or headman, who must settle disputes in consultation with a group of elders. The headman is usually the oldest and supposedly the wisest. All the people of the village, however, make known their views, and arguments are often long and loud.

Although men have the main power in a compound or village and women are not allowed to attend some ceremonies and council meetings, the women know how to make themselves heard. They often have their own ways of dealing out justice. A character in the novel *I Saw the Sky Catch Fire* by T. Obinkaram Echewa tells a tale about a man who had beaten his wife cruelly. A group of women were so angry at his conduct that they marched over to his hut, surrounded him, threw him down on the ground, and all sat on him to shame him in front of the other men.

In the compounds a man may have several wives. To a Westerner this might seem to be asking for trouble, with quarreling and jealousy among the wives. Strangely enough, many women in these compounds get along quite well. The senior wife often chooses the younger ones, and the wives often get together to boss the husband. They look upon the situation more as sharing the work than sharing the husband and would feel sorry for a woman who had to do the cooking, cleaning, gardening, and child raising all by herself. Women who are unhappy with their marriages often just pull up stakes and go back to their own families. Ties to one's own blood relations are usually much

Women in a compound share the work of pounding grain.

stronger than those between husband and wife. For both men and women, the strongest ties are with those of their own age group.

Life in a compound can be very noisy, and loneliness is unknown. Anthropologists who have lived in traditional compounds to study the customs have found it difficult to get time alone to work on their notes. The villagers have been unable to understand why anyone would actually want to be alone. They say such things as "All work is better in company," or "A man sits alone only to plot evil." Banishment to live alone away from the village is an extreme punishment.

MARRIAGE

Although a woman may decide to leave her husband and return to her family, she may not be welcomed back unless she has a good reason for having left. The husband pays a price—in goods and/or money—to her family when she becomes a bride. If he has not mistreated her, he will expect the payment to be returned if she leaves him.

In many countries the bride is supposed to bring a dowry—of goods or money—to her husband and his family. Nigeria is one of the countries where the man is expected to come up with a "bride price."

Muslims are allowed by their religion to have four wives. In old-style rural compounds men want several wives to help do the work of the compound and to provide many children. Rich Muslims may have more than one wife, not to do work but to show that they are wealthy enough to afford them. Many well-educated, Westernized Muslim men today may choose to have just one wife, while well-educated women are not likely to want another woman around.

According to old customs, women did not have much say in whom they married—and they still don't in some places. In the traditional ways of living, women get married in their teens. One of the older wives is responsible for looking after the younger one and helping her adjust. That's one good thing about a compound: support is built in, whereas in modern Western society some people spend quite a lot of money finding "support groups."

Because brides are valuable, families see to it that their daughters are attractive and well-trained for marriage. In different societies, of course, ideas of attractiveness vary. The kind of skinny models seen in Western fashion magazines would not be admired in Nigeria. Not so very long ago, for instance, in the Calabar region, there used to be a "fattening ceremony." Young girls between the ages of sixteen and eighteen were kept in a special house for two to twelve months to be specially fed to achieve the well-rounded figures that were most admired.

Modern women in Lagos

Modern educated women, of course, now have careers and are choosy about whom they marry. The "bride price" a man pays may be a sum of money to set the woman up in business. Women in villages have always sold such things as food and cloth at markets or at waysides but town- and city-dwelling educated women work in offices or at professions. They often are in no hurry to get married.

CHILDREN

People in compounds relate to their own age groups because that is how life is organized from childhood on. Children spend most of their time together, the older ones looking after the younger. Chores are shared with one's age group. In the rural areas, people want many children to help with the family farms and, when they grow up, to look after their elders. In remote places where modern medical treatment is not easily available—or

A child with his grandfather

is not trusted—many children do not live long, so having a large family ensures that enough offspring will survive.

Although children are valued, they are not spoiled. They may hang around and listen to what is going on in the adult world, but they are not allowed to interrupt, and a crying child will be removed from a group by another child. Children are expected to respect their elders, and parents, although demanding, are seldom harsh. It is not just a child's parents who keep him or her in order; any adult can join in teaching a child good behavior. You might think it would crush a child's spirit to have so many people telling him or her what to do all the time, but then, where do all those independent-minded Nigerians come from? Maybe knowing that the whole community is interested in you is a good start in life.

Life for Nigerian children is, of course, one of great contrasts. There are village children who help on farms, who sell such

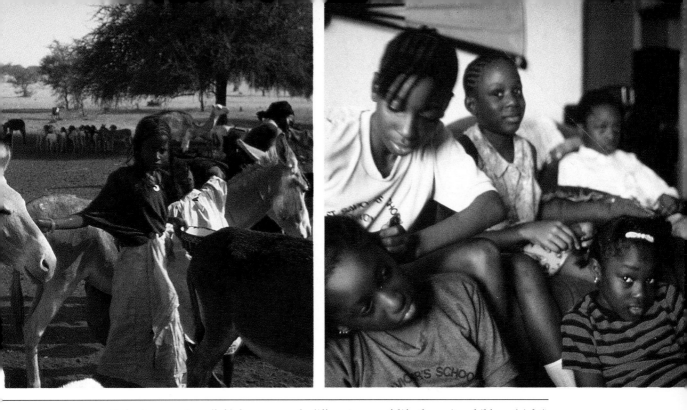

Fulani youngsters (left) have a much different way of life than city children (right).

things as fruit to travelers at wayside stops, or who help tend cattle in hot, dry areas. They may get very little, if any, schooling. There are children in towns and cities who live lives not very different from your own: going to school, watching television, playing games. Soccer is the favorite sport. In 1985 the Nigerian "Baby Eagles" won the soccer World Cup for under-sixteens at the Commonwealth games. Chris Okoye, an Igbo, plays in the United States for the National Football League. Teenagers, of course, are mad about music and dancing.

Speaking of teenagers, the Fulani seem to have worked out a good system for father-son relationships. A Fulani father, summoning his son from a group of friends, will do it in such a way that he does not seem to be ordering the boy as if he were a servant. The boy will respond with just enough delay to show that he is a free person, but fast enough to show that he respects his father.

Schoolchildren in Lagos

EDUCATION

The nature of many compounds changed with the arrival of the Christian missionaries. Churches and schools were built. Only one wife per man became the rule. Leadership of the community passed from men wise in the ways of the old spirit world to those educated in the ways of the world far beyond village life. The author Soyinka's father was such a man.

As education spread and people ventured forth to take jobs in the civil service, business, and the professions, the numbers living in towns and cities grew, and houses and apartments were built. Still the idea of community and ties to kinfolk endured.

Education is one method that different governments have used to encourage the idea of national unity. After independence the states took over the running of primary and secondary schools and of teacher-training and technical colleges. In 1976 the federal government set up universal primary education and made free secondary education available in 1979, although many students continued to leave school after the six primary years.

General Gowon—who did so much to settle the country after the Biafran War—took several steps to try to build a sense of Nigeria's being one nation. He put all universities under federal control and set up an examination board to establish standards of admission for all of them. He introduced a university course called Nigerian Heritage Studies to give students a feeling of patriotism. He formed a National Youth Service Corps to let students spend a year of service in parts of the country other than their own. He set up "unity schools," in which younger students from different ethnic groups and states could study together.

In 1966 there were five universities, including those at Lagos and Ibadan, that were run by the federal government. In 1975 the government took over the state universities at Ife, Benin, Nsukka, and Zaria. By 1979 there were thirteen universities, including those at Kano, Sokoto, and Jos. When the oil money was flowing, many other state universities were planned; but when the money ran out, buildings could not be completed. There also has been a teacher shortage at all levels of education. A great many Nigerians complete their higher education abroad in Great Britain, Europe, or the United States.

In education, as in laws and customs, Muslims follow the teachings of their own religion at all levels.

EATING, DRINKING, AND MAKING MERRY

Nigerian food is very spicy. It uses a variety of the kinds of hot peppers that bring tears to your eyes. A meal may consist of sauces made from different peppers or from peanuts. Into these

Left: Pieces of spiced meat are cooked over a charcoal fire.   Right: Fresh produce in an Ibadan market includes yams and the much-loved hot red peppers.

one dips chunks of thick porridgelike paste, rolling them, with the right hand, into balls. This basic starch is made from the root of the cassava melon or from the seeds of millet grass. In poor village areas, these roots or seeds are pounded into grain by the women. The process takes hours, so it is no wonder that women don't mind having extra wives to help! Rice is substituted as the dipping ingredient where it is grown locally or where people can afford the imported variety. Stews of fish, chicken, or various meats are also popular. The yam is a plentiful vegetable, and in some areas its harvest is an occasion for celebration. Mangoes and plantains, a kind of banana, are favorite fruits, and kola nuts are much valued. They are often given as gifts, and when chewed, they have the same effect as coffee and so are used by those who need to stay awake.

The most popular soft drink is so strongly flavored with ginger that it burns the throat of any foreigner not used to it. Beer is very common and is drunk even by Muslims, who are not supposed to drink alcohol. In villages it is brewed by the women, and in some areas, they sell it to their husbands. There are also thirty commercial breweries in Nigeria, producing beers judged to be excellent. Then there is palm wine, juice from the palm oil tree in which fermentation occurs naturally. In the oil-rich days, Nigeria imported more champagne than any other country in the world.

Nigerians are always ready for a celebration. A wedding, for instance, leads to days of visiting with in-laws, exchanging gifts, and feasting. The naming of a child—which should be done on the twenty-eighth day of its life—is another occasion for gatherings of friends and relatives. Some African names have very special meanings; for instance, parents who have had several girls and then have a boy may call the child *Obiajulu*, meaning "the mind is now at rest." Should they have another girl, they might call her *Nwanyidmma*, "a girl is also good," or, not quite so enthusiastically, *Nwanyibuife*, "a female is also something."

Gift giving is important in Nigerian life and is common even among poor people. Between those of equal station in life, the one receiving the gift will be expected to return a gift of equal value at some time. A gift should always be received with both hands to show proper appreciation. To take a gift with just one hand indicates that it is not good enough. Men of wealth give to the less fortunate to show their superior position, that they are "big men." This is expected of them. Unfortunately, this habit of giving and expecting gifts has had a serious result: some people expect money for favors—in other words, bribery, one of the wrongs that Nigerians are always complaining about. It makes life quite difficult for most people; for instance, even after a person has passed the driving test, it may be necessary to bribe a government official before the driver's license is handed over.

Guests at a wedding reception (above) get up to dance.
Traditional musicians perform in the open air (below).

Chapter 8

"BRING YOUR
DANCING SHOES"

"Be sure to bring your dancing shoes" is the advice in one guidebook for the traveler to Nigeria. All social events—village celebrations, weddings, naming of infants, even funerals—are accompanied by music and dancing. In the cities, ballroom and disco dancing are popular.

In Western countries people often sit quietly listening to jazz with maybe just a little toe tapping or head waggling. In Nigeria people get up and dance in response to the beat. This is what they are meant to do; the musicians would be insulted if people didn't dance.

TRADITIONAL MUSIC

Traditional music is totally dependent on rhythm—the beat. All instruments are native and made with local materials such as gourds, animal skins, and horns. The drum is the most important. Drums may be round, as Western ones are, or they may be shaped like cylinders, goblets, or hourglasses. The skins stretched across the drums are most often goatskin, and it is said that this is appropriate because the goat is the most talkative animal and the drum is used to communicate a mood or a feeling.

Talking drums (left) and a variety of wind instruments (right)

Nigerian drumming can be tremendously exciting. Wole Soyinka, in his play *The Jewel and the Lion*, uses drums as an important part of the action. In this play a young woman has two suitors. One, a young man in love with progress, offers her a modern, Westernized life. The other, a cunning old chief, offers her a traditional life as the last and, he says, the most valued of his several wives. The thrilling drumming and dancing at the play's end make the pleasures of civilization offered by the young man seem pale and dull by contrast. The old man is letting the drums "talk for him."

Traditional music also uses wind instruments, such as flutes, made from gourds, shells, or wood. As none of these instruments has a scale, the music produced has only a subtle melody but wonderful changes of rhythm.

Traditional music marks different situations, each having its own distinct kind of music. There is special music, too, for different groups: for women, young people, warriors, and so on.

Many kinds of popular music can be heard in Nigeria.

POPULAR MUSIC

Popular music is a favorite all over West Africa, especially in Nigeria, and it reflects the many different influences that have reached the country in the twentieth century. There are Latin-American strains, like the conga and rumba; echoes of ballads brought in by sailors from around the world; Western "swing" music picked up from Western allied troops during World War II; calypso from the West Indies; and modern American jazz, soul, and rock. Some of the music has come full circle. Much of the Latin-American, West Indian, and United States music was influenced by Nigerian people—who were brought to these countries as slaves.

"HIGHLIFE"

The most modern form of popular music is known as "highlife," which became immensely popular in southern Nigeria.

It was developed for ballroom dancing by "high-class" patrons of hotels and dance halls. It is played from written music by paid musicians who wear Western dress and sing in English. Saxophones, trumpets, and trombones are featured in these bands, which are no longer popular with younger people.

JUJU

Juju music is the favorite of the younger generation in Nigeria. It originated among the Yoruba and is special to Nigeria, and not much played in other West African countries. Juju bands differ greatly from highlife ones. The musicians do not get paid a regular salary but take up collections from their listeners. They usually wear Yoruba dress and sing in a native language. Although guitars and other Western instruments are used, the heart of these bands is the "talking" drum, and the songs are about local people and affairs. During the Biafran War, highlife musicians fled from Lagos to Biafra, leaving juju musicians to take over the city. Although juju does not have much of a following elsewhere in Africa, in other parts of the world it is well known. Two of the most popular groups internationally are King Sunny Ade and His African Beats and Chief Commander Ebenezer Obey and His Inter-Reformers Band.

AFRO-BEAT

This music was developed by Fela Anikulapo-Kuti, known simply as Fela. He traveled to the United States in the 1960s and became a fan of American musician James Brown. He blended Brown's jazz with African music to produce Afro-Beat.

Fela without makeup (far left), and performing (left) in concert.

These bands use Western guitars, trumpets, saxophones, and electric pianos, but the drum is still all-important and the total sound is unmistakably African. As in juju, the songs are social comments.

Fela's songs are always highly critical of politicians. The people love them, but the politicians don't. Fela was exiled to Ghana from 1978 to 1980, and then in 1985 he was framed by the government on a currency-smuggling charge and given a five-year prison sentence. So much loud protest arose from his many admirers that the authorities set him free in 1986. Other famous Afro-Beat musicians are Sonny Okosun and his "Jungle Rock" music and a group called Ghetto Blaster.

There is international interest in African music, and recordings can be bought in the United States, Great Britain, and Europe. People from other countries go to Nigeria to study the music and its meaning for the people. This study is called *ethnomusicology*, and the people who practice it write books and articles about their findings. They are usually professors or advanced students hoping to become professors. Their studies often include learning to play African drums and joining in bands and doing various dances.

Chapter 9

A WORLD OF
FORM AND COLOR

In 1897 the British, bent on settling an ongoing state of warfare, invaded Benin City, which had for centuries been the capital city of a powerful kingdom that once extended as far as present-day Lagos. When they arrived the British were horrified to find that a ceremony involving human sacrifice had just taken place. However, they were amazed to find in the king's palace some two thousand magnificent bronze statues, which they proceeded to make off with.

When people of the Western world saw these treasures, they were astounded. It was the first time Westerners realized that Africans other than ancient Egyptians could produce such treasures, and museums throughout Europe rushed to buy them. Nigerian art is now among the most highly prized in the world, and it is forbidden to take the oldest, most valuable pieces out of the country. Many fine artists work in Nigeria today, and local businessmen, officials, and professionals collect their work.

The Nigerian flair for art and for crafts can be seen everywhere, and many beautiful objects can be bought in markets around the country. Although not everything is of the highest quality, none of

Opposite page: A bronze plaque, thought to have been produced in the sixteenth century, shows a king and his court.

Huge calabash gourds are cut into bowls and decorated with hand carvings (left); a man carves small figurines from thorn wood (right); glass bottles and jars are recycled into attractive beads (inset).

it is mass-produced. There are wood carvings, masks, decorative knives, painted gourds, colorful fabrics, and jewelry—from elaborately carved wooden bracelets to necklaces cleverly made of glass recycled from coke or beer bottles.

THE MASTER ARTISTS

Among the most admired art in Nigeria—much of it centuries old—is that of the Yoruba and the Igbo. As does all enduring art, it expresses how these people viewed their world and what their values were. Artists were always honored. For instance, the Yoruba, in a song of praise of hunters, included these lines:

Not the brave alone, they also praise those who

know how to shape images in wood or compose a song.

Some of the treasures of early Yoruba art are beautiful terra-cotta heads. They are obviously portraits of real people and date

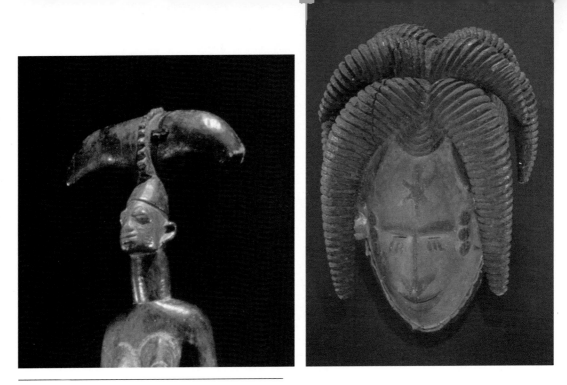

Hand-carved works from Yoruba (left) and Igbo craftspeople (right) are greatly admired.

back to the tenth century. The ancient Greek sculptures tell us that the Greeks valued regular—what we sometimes call "classic"—features. We know from Yoruba sculptures that the Yoruba valued character, for the heads show wisdom and strength. They believed in the middle ground. People should not be too short or too tall, not too ugly but not too good-looking. (Many legends tell of beautiful people turning into skeletons!) Modern Yoruba still say "Beauty comes to an end, character is forever."

Apart from the portrait heads, there are older carved and bronze figures that are not realistic but symbolic. For instance, many figures are shown with open hands held out, standing for the virtue of generosity, which was considered all-important. Generosity and hospitality are still highly prized in Nigeria.

Other figures relate to various gods. Such symbols as feathers, iron tools, palm leaves, and *cowrie* (sea snail) shells refer to powers belonging to different gods believed to control the

Useful objects produced in Nigeria—a footstool, a clay pot, and a leather handbag—are also designed to be ornamental.

elements and to bring good or evil. Charms using similar designs are still kept to ward off evil by some modern Nigerians and by some descendants of Nigerian slaves in the New World—in the Caribbean, Brazil, Cuba, and New York City.

Much of the great early Nigerian art is to be found in objects that were useful as well as ornamental. Because the Yoruba were early city dwellers, they had more wealth and more household goods than rural people. They had intricately carved pillars at the entrances to houses, terra-cotta or metal pots for liquids, masks for special ceremonies, and elaborate stools. During the same early period as the Yoruba, the Igbo also produced terra-cotta and bronze bowls that many consider to be of finer quality than those of the Yoruba. Igbo masks, too, are judged by some to be more imaginative, varied, and "sculptural."

A particularly interesting kind of small carved figure is the *ibeji*. This represents the cult of twins. The Yoruba, for some reason,

*Two artists make intricate carvings on this door,
which is fashioned from a single sheet of wood.*

have more twins than any other people in the world, and twins are considered good luck. However, should one twin or both die, a carver makes an image of the dead child or children; such images are treasured and treated as if still part of the family.

THE TRADITION GOES ON

There are many artists today who work in ways that often borrow (or adapt) much from the Yoruba and other Nigerian traditional artistic styles. Among the most famous are Olowe of Ise, a master wood carver in the more traditional sense, and the Nigerian-born Sokari Douglas Camp, now working in London and noted for her splendid, contemporary metal sculpture. In North America, interest in the art of their ancestors inspired African-American artists during the Harlem Renaissance of the 1920s and the civil rights movement of the 1960s.

A bronze leopard from the fifteenth century

Nigerian and other African art has long been part of the international scene. Major museums have their own collections and hold special exhibits. There is a National Museum of African Art in Washington, D.C., and New York has the Museum for African Art. Galleries around the world including many in Nigeria itself compete for the finest pieces to sell to private collectors, and magazines and journals are devoted to the subject. There are books in your library with more pictures of the wonderful works you've been reading about.

DRESSING UP

Much Nigerian clothing is a form of art in itself, using wonderful colorful fabric and handsome designs. Nigerians enjoy dressing up and often spend a large part of their income on

Loose, lightweight robes keep these herders cool and comfortable.

clothes. People may buy several outfits to carry them through the several days of a wedding, birth, or funeral ceremony. Such outfits are not bought "off-the-rack," but are specially made in traditional styles, often elaborately beaded, brightly colored, and costing more than the buyer can really afford. But being well dressed at such ceremonies is seen as a mark of respect.

Although there are those who wear Western clothing, African styles make sense in such a hot climate. For both men and women, there are long, loose robes. Men wear these robes over lightweight trousers. Women may wear a loose top and a length of cotton used as a wraparound skirt. Girls wear simple cotton dresses and boys, loose shirts and shorts. In rural areas, children wear little or nothing, and in really remote places, the adults don't wear much either. The cattle herders, for instance, wrap themselves in a long cloth, much like a toga.

*A variety of fabric is available in the markets (opposite page)
such as imported striped cotton (left) and handwoven robes (right).*

Given the climate, cottons and muslins are much favored, and
these usually are boldly patterned with effects achieved by *batik*, a
waxing process; or *tie-dyeing*, which you've probably seen on T-
shirts; or block printing.

Other beautiful designs are created by an ancient method called
narrow strip weaving. Such weaving is traditionally done by men.
As the name suggests, strips of cloth are woven on a narrow-
gauge loom, and the strips are sewn together in a striking striped
pattern. Some ceremonial garments use as many as one hundred
narrow strips. Such a robe is too heavy for many tastes, and
recently people have come to prefer imported striped cotton. In
fact, quite a lot of fabric is now imported.

Much Nigerian clothing is designed with an eye to how it will
look in motion as the people dance. In particular, there are
wonderful Yoruba ceremonial robes made with several layers of
different colored fabrics so that in a dance, the swirling colors
give the effect of a spinning top. These robes are so beautiful that
examples often form part of art exhibits.

Chapter 10

IMPORTANT PLACES

THE CITY-STATE OF LAGOS

This important port and business center is in the southwest of the country and is the former capital. Nigerians feel about Lagos rather as Americans do about New York City. Those who don't live there consider it to be a wicked and dangerous place; those who live there think that those who don't are hicks. Young people eager to get ahead want to go there to seek their fortunes, figuring that "if you can make it there, you'll make it anywhere," as the song says about New York. Lagos, however, has not made itself into a tourist attraction and it is unlikely that "I ♥ Lagos" buttons would sell well.

All over Nigeria, as in other parts of the world, people have flocked to cities from rural areas. The growth of Lagos has been particularly astonishing. In 1970, the population was around 800,000; by 1990, it was almost 1,500,000. It is thought that by 2025, it will probably be one of the five largest cities in the world. It is the largest city in all of black Africa, and its population is largely Yoruban.

As you can imagine, Lagos has all the problems of most modern, overcrowded urban centers, including a high crime rate.

Opposite page: A view of Lagos harbor filled with pleasure craft

Apartments are crowded into a congested area of Lagos Island.
Inset above: Visitors attend a fun fair featuring inflatable houses.

Visitors are warned to beware of thieves and cabdrivers who overcharge. Visitors also are warned that Lagos has some of the world's worst traffic jams. It can take three hours to drive seven miles (eleven kilometers). Nigeria is famous for free enterprise, and Lagos is flooded with street traders who surround stopped cars trying to sell all kinds of merchandise to passengers. (In New York more and more street traders also are to be found, and a lot of them are from West Africa—some probably from Lagos!)

Still, in spite of the disadvantages, people still come to Lagos to try their luck because good jobs are to be found there. Lagos is more closely linked to the rest of the world than other Nigerian cities. All major European countries have embassies here, as do Australia, Canada, Japan, and the United States. There are several major banks, including the Bank of America.

The main part of Lagos consists of Lagos Island—the "downtown" district—Ikoyi Island, and Victoria Island, where the

Opposite page: A night view of an apartment building on Victoria Island (top inset), the National Stadium, and part of the highway system in downtown Lagos (bottom inset)

The National Theater and a carved door (inset) in the oba's palace

best hotels and houses are. There also are good but, of course, crowded beaches.

There are lots of things to do in Lagos. It is famous for the exciting music to be heard and danced to in hotels and clubs. Because of all the foreigners who come here on business, there are all sorts of restaurants—Nigerian, French, Chinese, and Indian. And there are hamburgers for those who don't like adventurous eating.

On the outskirts of Lagos is the National Theater, built in 1976, which shows plays, dances, and films. Here, too, is the National Museum, displaying some of the Benin bronzes and beautiful wood carvings for which Nigeria is world famous. The museum includes a craft center, where visitors not only can buy carvings and decorative fabrics but can watch artists creating them. Fabrics, baskets, jewelry, and wood carvings are to be found in markets around the city.

Interesting buildings include the palace of the *oba*, or king, of

Ibadan (left) is also a very crowded city. The Ibadan Zoo (above), like zoos everywhere, is a popular place to visit.

Lagos, built in the eighteenth century. The oldest part has the unusual combination of mud walls and bronze pillars.

ALSO IN THE SOUTH

Ibadan, northwest of Lagos, once the largest city in Nigeria, is now only half the size of Lagos, but that means that it is still pretty crowded. It is not generally considered to be a very attractive city to visit, but because it is a Yoruba city and the

University buildings at Ibadan

Yoruba value education highly, it has an excellent university. There is also an important research center, the International Institute of Tropical Agriculture.

Halfway between Ibadan and Lagos is Ife, the place where human life began, according to Yoruba legend. Here is the palace of the oni, who considers himself to be the ruler of all the Yoruba—those in Nigeria and in other African countries, as well as the descendants of the Yoruba who live anywhere in the world. He often makes journeys to visit people in faraway places such as the West Indies. Each oni is said to be a direct descendant of the original father of the human race. In the past, onis were warlords, then political leaders under the British colonial system, and,

A contemporary mosaic in a building in Kaduna and the
shrine to Oshun, the river goddess (right)

always, religious leaders. The present oni is also a very wealthy
businessman who rides around in a large limousine. He even has
a media director, and videos of the oni conducting religious
ceremonies and traveling around on official business are available
to his followers.

Near here is the town of Oshogbo, famous not only for the
shrine to the river goddess, Oshun, but for being an artists' center.
Many of these artists produce beautiful mosaics that are
commissioned for buildings from palaces to banks to hotels.
Examples can be seen in both the National Museum and the
National Theater in Lagos.

The cultural museum in Benin City

Benin City, east of Lagos, dates back to the tenth century. It was long the center of great power. The museum has samples of bronze work as well as terra-cotta pottery, masks, ornamental doorways, and ivory carvings. Nearby is the oba's palace, where unimpressive outside mud walls hide a wonderfully decorated interior.

East of Benin City in a thickly populated area lies Onitsha, the site of the largest market in all of West Africa. Many parts of the city, including this huge market, were destroyed in the Biafran War but have been largely rebuilt. There is also a different kind of market that is surely unique. Authors flock here—ordinary people who may be shopkeepers, farmers, or taxi drivers—all selling their own cheaply produced books on all sorts of topics. Romances and plays about marriage are particularly popular, and the writers eagerly promote their own books, promising hours of entertainment. Many writers all over the world who have trouble getting published might think it is not such a bad idea.

An aerial view of Port Harcourt

Port Harcourt, in the southeast on the Gulf of Guinea, was built originally to export coal but grew enormously more important as an oil port. Some 95 percent of Nigeria's wealth is centered here, and it houses more foreigners than any other place except Lagos. It is a very expensive place to live.

THE CENTER

During the oil-boom years, the government decided to build a new capital at Abuja. (In the early twentieth century, this had been a stronghold of fierce bandits.) The site was chosen as part of the effort to unite the country, for it is in the exact center of Nigeria. Its location is meant to show that no one part of the country is more important than any other part. This city, then, was created in what many thought was the middle of nowhere, carved out of the bush. The president's headquarters are in Abuja

*Some animals living in the Yankari Game Reserve are
waterbucks (left), baboons (center), and elephants (right).*

and all major government ministries will eventually be located
here, but when the oil boom was over, construction slowed down;
many buildings still are not completed. The original planners
aimed at accommodation for 1.5 million people, but by the end of
1992 only some 400,000 were living there. Great things,
however, are still hoped for, and a 1,000-room Hilton Hotel awaits
the time when Abuja will finally fulfill the dream of its creators.
A lot of Nigerians believe that much too much money has been
wasted in building this city.

Jos, in the central plateau region, has the advantage of a
comparatively cool climate and pleasant scenery. It has a famous
museum that includes a zoo and some of the most beautiful
pottery in the country. There is also a museum of architecture
with full-scale reproductions of buildings from all major regions of
Nigeria—from mosques to thatched village huts to a replica of the
wall that once surrounded the ancient city of Kano. Another
attraction near Jos is the Wildlife Game Preserve, where animals

Left: Workmen dip cloth in dye pits to produce Kano cloth. Above: The green dome and twin minarets of Kano's central mosque

such as elephants, lions, and hippos can be observed from tourists' cars. The pelicans there are said to be so tame that they wander into the reserve's restaurants looking for handouts. Zoos and game preserves in Nigeria are not just for visitors from abroad. Most Nigerians do not meet wild animals in their daily life. There are camels in the north, crocodiles and hippopotamuses in some rivers, snakes in forest areas, and monkeys and chimpanzees in many places. Common birds include quail, vultures, kites, and gray parrots.

THE NORTH

Kano, in the center of the northern region, is one of the former Hausa city-states. It is the oldest major city in West Africa and the third-largest city in Nigeria. A stronghold of Islamic learning for centuries, it has a famous central mosque that on Friday draws as many as fifty thousand Muslims to midday prayer. Next to the

Freshly painted houses in Kano

mosque is the emir's palace, and attached to that is a museum built as long ago as the fifteenth century. Although it is a religious center, Kano also is—and always has been—a place of business. It caters to those who come there as tourists or on business with hotels, restaurants, and nightclubs. It also has the largest city zoo in Nigeria.

Katsina, northwest of Kano, still preserves much of its old customs and appearance. Special sights include the old wall and the Gold Minaret. On the outskirts, old Hausa burial mounds can be seen. The city is most famous for the spectacular Durbar festival, held each year at the end of Ramadan. The main event is a procession of magnificently dressed men in coats of armor and scarlet turbans topped with plumed copper helmets, riding on horses decorated from nose to tail. The local emir, dressed in white, rides under a silver-embroidered parasol, surrounded by

Participants in the annual Durbar festival

horsemen dressed in blue. He is followed by traditional wrestlers and lute players. As the horsemen go thundering by it is a colorful and awesome sight, and thousands flock to see it.

Sokoto, in the far northwest corner of the country, also has an impressive festival to mark the end of Ramadan. This festival features ornately dressed horsemen and processions of musicians who wend their way to the palace of the local sultan, who is the religious leader of the Nigerian Muslims. The famous "Moroccan leather" really comes from here. Many handmade leather items can be bought in street markets in Sokoto and there is also a government-run factory.

Although Nigeria has not tried to attract tourists in the way African countries such as Kenya have, many foreign visitors go there to conduct business, to study, to work, and just to travel around and meet the ever-fascinating people.

Chapter 11

VOICES FROM NIGERIA

Most of our knowledge of Nigerian history comes from outsiders: from the records of missionaries, traders, explorers, and colonial administrators. Scholars studying various Nigerian ways of living, travelers telling of their adventures, people doing business in the country, all report on conditions they find. In earlier times the record of what had happened in various regions was passed from generation to generation by word of mouth: that is, oral history. The many Nigerian historians writing in recent times include Adiele Afigbo, C. Ifemesia, and Walter Ofonagoro.

Much of what Westerners know about Nigeria has not been learned from historians but from poets, playwrights, and novelists. Nigeria overflows with them—more than any other African country. There are so many poets that it is possible to get a degree in Nigerian poetry at the University of Ibadan. Through fiction and poetry, we often can learn more about a country than we can from so-called facts.

Some of the writers best known outside Nigeria write in English, so their stories, plays, and poems are known to a wide world of readers. These writers tell tales that were told to them as

Wole Soyinka

children. They recount legends and describe customs. They tell of the struggle between old and new ways. Those who have been abroad—and they are many—tell of their experiences as black people in countries that are largely white. They also write of the things they find wrong about their country today. The true spirit of Nigeria is to be found in this splendid literature.

Among writers best known in the Western world is Wole Soyinka, the Nobel Prize winner. His most famous works include *Aké: The Years of Childhood,* his wonderful account of growing up in a Yoruba compound with his beloved father, a much-respected teacher who could be both kind and, when necessary, stern; and with his memorable mother—the "Wild Christian"—who not only could deal with her own children but could teach good behavior to others who were causing too much trouble to their own mothers. (If any of her children felt neglected or unjustly treated, they could always find someone else's mother to console them.)

Soyinka also wrote a recent book about his father, *Isárá: A Voyage Around "Essay."* This tells of what life was like in a small Nigerian town in the 1930s; of the struggle between the desire to honor tradition and the desire to take advantage of the education and other opportunities offered by the British.

Soyinka, born in 1934, graduated from the universities of Ibadan, Nigeria, and Leeds, England. He worked at the famous Royal Court Theatre in London, first as a play reader and then as a playwright, and had his first three plays produced there in 1958 and 1959. He returned to Nigeria in 1960 as a university teacher, also writing and acting in more plays. (He has written twenty of them.) His first novel, *The Interpreters*, was written in 1965 and told of the hopes of young Nigerians for the future of the country. His fearless writing about what he thought was wrong with the government landed him in jail, briefly in 1965 and then for two years, 1967 and 1968, for his support of Igbos of Biafra during the Nigerian Civil War. In prison he wrote poetry and a second novel. On his release he wrote a famous account of his imprisonment, *The Man Died*, which contains a sentence that most Nigerians would agree with: "The man dies in all who keep silent in the face of tyranny."

In 1972 Soyinka left Nigeria, traveling and teaching in other parts of Africa, Europe, and the United States. He returned to Nigeria in 1976. He has been a teacher, a literary critic, and an editor. Always, he has fought against the injustices he sees, often using humor and ridicule as weapons.

Equally well-known around the world is Chinua Achebe, an Igbo. His novel *Things Fall Apart*, published in 1958, was the first Nigerian novel to be classed as world literature. It has been

Chinua Achebe

translated into French, German, Italian, Spanish, Hebrew, Russian, Czech, and Hungarian. It is about an Igbo clan between 1880 and 1900, the period just before and shortly after the white colonists arrived. It tells how that community set its rules for living in harmony and of the downfall of a man whose pride and ambition caused him to break these rules.

Achebe's other novels include *No Longer at Ease*, *Arrow of God*, *A Man of the People*, and his latest, *Anthills of the Savannah*. This latest one is about an overambitious military leader of an imaginary African country and two friends of his younger days who helped put him in power but who now know he will destroy them. In spite of its dark theme, the book is full of humor and hope for better days. It has great portraits of the contrasting types to be found in Nigeria, from simple pidgin-speaking people to well-educated professionals.

Achebe was graduated from University College, Ibadan. He worked in broadcasting and became a professor at the University of Nigeria Nsukka. He is well known in the United States and has been professor of English at the Universities of Massachusetts and Connecticut.

It would need a thick book to tell about all the Nigerian writers, but here are a few whose works can be read in English.

J.P. Clark, from the Niger delta area, founded a poetry magazine, *The Horn,* while attending University College, Ibadan. He taught for many years at Lagos University and is both poet and playwright.

Aig Higo, born in western Nigeria, has been a teacher as well as a poet and is managing director of the Nigerian branch of the British publishing house, Heinemann.

Gabriel Okara, from the delta area, has written poems and plays for radio and one novel, *The Voice.* He was also the first editor of the newspaper *Nigerian Tide.*

Ken Saro-Wiwa, whose novels include *Prisoner of Jebs* and *Sojaboy,* writes and also produces a television sitcom called *Basi and Company* about get-rich-quick schemes. It has an audience of thirty million.

T. Obinkaram Echewa has degrees from three American universities—Notre Dame, Columbia, and the University of Pennsylvania. His most recent novel, *I Saw the Sky Catch Fire,* tells of the dilemma of a young Nigerian torn between his longing to go on studying at an American university and his duty to return to Nigeria to look after not only his own wife and child but the family compound of his ancestors.

Many of Nigeria's writers are women. The best known is probably Flora Nwapa. Others include Buchi Emecheta, who weaves traditional tales from Igbo culture into her novels.

From the writings of these and many other talented authors, both the old and the new Nigeria can be seen in all its diversity.

WHAT DOES THE FUTURE HOLD?

Other voices are constantly raised in Nigeria's many newspapers, calling attention to the country's various problems. Like citizens of most countries, Nigerians do not like other people to criticize them. But in spite of years of military rule, the press has mostly remained free, and in true democratic fashion, Nigeria is quick to criticize itself. People write letters to editors complaining of crime, inefficiency, and other ills. Newspapers are the most outspoken in Africa. A typical headline that ran a few years ago was "It wouldn't be Nigeria if it worked." The determination persists, however, to make it work.

Education is the key to Nigeria's future. Children (above) up to fifteen years old receive free education. Adults are encouraged to take literacy classes (opposite page).

Nigeria has been described as black Africa's best hope. With all
the differences in culture, language, and religion, it has since the
Biafran War avoided the tragic, long-drawn-out civil wars that
have shattered so many African countries. Foreigners who go
there may wonder how what seem to them to be overwhelming
problems can ever be solved. But they marvel at the spirit of the
people. An American journalist, Blaine Harden, who was head of
the *Washington Post* bureau in sub-Saharan Africa in the late 1980s,
was one who recognized this spirit. "It seems that things are often
about to fall apart," he wrote, adding that Nigerians were
nevertheless managing to meld themselves into one nation and
that "against all odds, things come together."

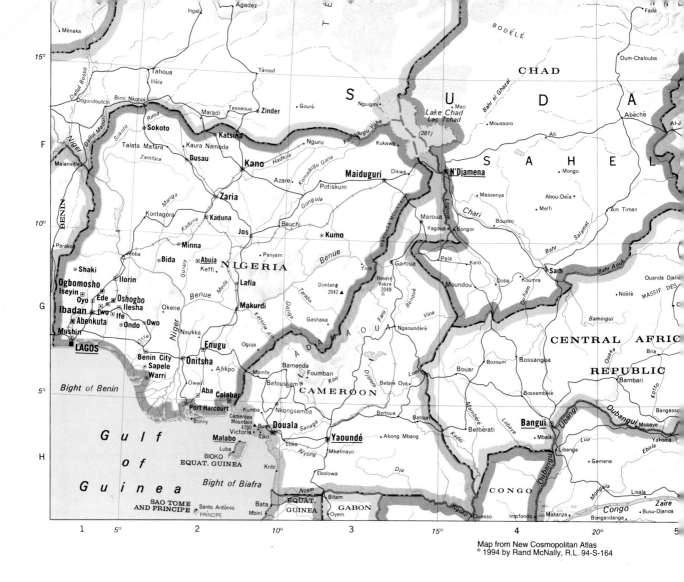

Map from New Cosmopolitan Atlas
© 1994 by Rand McNally, R.L. 94-S-164

MAP KEY

		Gulf of Guinea	G1, H1, H2	Komadugu Yobe, *river*	F3	Onitsha	G2
Aba	G2	Gurara, *river*	G2	Kontagora	F2	Oshogbo	G1
Abeokuta	G1	Gusau	F2	Kukawa	F3	Osse, *river*	G2
Abuja	G2	Hadejia, *river*	F2, F3	Kumo	F3	Owerri	G2
Afikpo	G2	Ibadan	G1	Lafia	G2	Owo	G2
Azare	F3	Ife	G1	Lagos	G1	Oyo	G1
Bauchi	F2	Ilesha	G1	Mada, *river*	G2	Panyam	G2
Benin City	G2	Ilorin	G1	Maiduguri	F3	Port Harcourt	H2
Benue, *river*	G2, G3	Iseyin	G1	Makurdi	G2	Potiskum	F3
Bida	G2	Iwo	G1	Mandara Mountains	F3, G3	Rima, *river*	F2
Bight of Benin	G1	Jebba	G1	Mariga, *river*	F2, G2	Sapele	G2
Bonny	H2	Jos	F2, G2	Minna	G2	Shaki	G1
Calabar	G2, H2	Kaduna	F2	Mushin	G1	Sokoto	F2
Dikwa	F3	Kaduna, *river*	F2, G2	Nguru	F3	Sokoto, *river*	F1, F2
Dimlang	G3	Kano	F2	Niger, *river*	F1, G1, G2, H2	Talata Mafara	F2
Donga, *river*	G3	Katsina	F2	Nsukka	G2	Taraba, *river*	G3
Ede	G1	Katsina Ala, *river*	G2	Ogbomosho	G1	Warri	G2
Enugu	G2	Kaura Namoda	F2	Ogoja	G2	Yola	G3
Gashaka	G3	Keffi	G2	Okene	G2	Zamfara, *river*	F1, F2
Gongola, *river*	F3	Komadugu Gana, *river*	F3	Ondo	G1	Zaria	F2

The central plateau in Nigeria

MINI-FACTS AT A GLANCE

GENERAL INFORMATION

Official Name: Federal Republic of Nigeria

Capital: Abuja (Federal Capital Territory); before 1991 the capital was Lagos. The president's headquarters are in Abuja and all major government ministries eventually will be located there.

Government: The last civilian government was overthrown in a military coup in November 1993. The military leader has often become head of state and of government—that is, when a civilian president is not holding office. The 1979 constitution allocates power between the federal and state governments and sets up a presidential form of government like the United States. The Nigerian legal system is based on English common law and consists of both state and federal courts. Judges of the Supreme Court (the highest court of appeal) must have knowledge of Islamic as well as English common law. For administrative purposes the country is divided into 30 states and one federal capital territory, Abuja.

Religion: The constitution does not support an official religion. The principal religious groups are Muslims, mostly Sunni, (almost 50 percent) and Christians (about 40 percent); some 10 percent of the population follows traditional beliefs. The Hausa people follow Islam and the Yoruba are mostly Christian.

Ethnic Composition: Almost all Nigerians are of black African descent. About 300 ethnic groups give the country a rich cultural diversity. The three largest groups are the Hausa (mostly in the north and northwest), the Yoruba (in the southwest), and the Igbo (in the southeast). The Kanuri (near Lake Chad) and the Tiv (in central Nigeria) are two other major ethnic groups. Hausa-Fulani is the largest sub-group of Hausa people.

Language: English is the official language and is taught in schools throughout the country. Most educated Nigerians speak English and it is the most widely used language. About 21 percent of the population speaks Hausa; followed by Yoruba, 20 percent; Igbo, 17 percent; and Fulani, 9 percent. Muslim Nigerians use Arabic for religious activities. People with little or no education use Nigerian-Pidgin, a combination of English and their native tongue.

National Flag: Officially adopted in 1960, the Nigerian flag is a vertical tricolor of green, white, and green stripes. The white stripe in the middle signifies peace and unity, and the green on both sides stands for agriculture.

National Emblem: The black shield in the middle of the emblem refers to the rich soil of the land. Two wide silver wavy lines make the letter Y in the middle of the shield, expressing the confluence of the Niger and Benue Rivers. Two white horses representing dignity stand on a green mound covered with wildflowers on both sides of the shield. An outstretched red eagle at the top of the shield represents strength; a yellow scroll carrying the national motto "Unity and Faith" appears at the bottom of the shield.

National Anthem: "Arise, O Compatriots"

National Calendar: Gregorian

Money: Nigerian naira (N) of 100 kobo is the official currency unit. In April 1995 one N was worth $0.05 in United States currency.

Membership in International Organizations: African Development Bank (AfDB), Economic Community of West African States (ECOWAS), Group of 77 (G-77), Nonaligned Movement (NAM), Organization of African Unity (OAU), Organization of the Islamic Conference (OIC), Organization of Petroleum Exporting Countries (OPEC), United Nations (UN) and several of its special agencies, World Tourism Organization (WTO)

Weights and Measures: The metric system is in force.

Population: 93,472,000 (1994 estimate); almost one-quarter of the sub-Saharan population of Africa lives in Nigeria. Nigeria is the most populous country in Africa; it ranks among the 10 most populous countries in the world; one in five Africans is Nigerian. Population density, 262 persons per sq. mi. (101 per sq km); 64 percent rural, 36 percent urban

Cities:

Lagos	1,444,000
Ibadan	1,362,000
Ogbomosho	694,400
Kano	641,200
Oshogbo	453,600
Ilorin	452,700
Abeokuta	406,500

Port Harcourt 389,900
Zaria 360,800
Ilesha 359,900
Onitsha 353,800
Enugu 300,700
(Population based on 1994 estimates.)

GEOGRAPHY

Border: Benin is to the west, Niger to the north, Chad to the northeast, Cameroon to the east and southeast, and the Gulf of Guinea is to the south.

Coastline: 478 mi. (769 km) along the Gulf of Guinea and the Bight (Bay) of Benin

Land: The landscape in Nigeria is varied. The northern savanna region is flat with tropical grass and stunted trees. The middle plateau region is the least populated area. The southern region has most of Nigeria's natural resources and is the most populous region. The coastal region is one of lagoons and swamps overgrown with mangrove trees. The central Jos Plateau and the northeastern Biu Plateau consist of extensive lava surfaces and are dotted with many extinct volcanoes. The Niger-Benue River basin occupies three-fifths of the country's land area. The Oyo-Yoruba upland is in the southwest and the Udi Plateau is in the southeast; the Adamawa highlands are along the eastern border. The Chad Basin of the interior drainage is in the extreme southeast. In the extreme north is the southern part of the Sahara desert.

Highest Point: Dimlang Peak (6,699 ft.; 2,042 m)

Lowest Point: Sea level along the coast

Rivers and Lakes: The Niger, the third largest river in Africa, enters Nigeria from the northwest and runs in a southeasterly direction; about one-third of its course of 2,600 mi. (4,200 km) is in Nigeria. Nigeria derives its name from the Niger River. The Benue is the major tributary of the Niger. Other rivers are the Sokoto, Kaduna, and Gongola. Lake Chad in the extreme northeast shrinks and expands significantly with the seasons; it is one of the world's largest sources of freshwater fish.

Forests: About one-sixth of the country's area is forested, but illegal deforestation is a major problem. Major trees are the African mahogany, iroko, African walnut, oil palm, and obeche; the baobab tree produces gourdlike fruit and the tamarind tree produces seeds that are used to flavor food and drinks. A mangrove swamp belt exists along the coast.

Wildlife: Only a few of the larger wild animals are found in the rain forests; they include gorillas, chimpanzees, baboons, and monkeys. Reptiles include crocodiles, lizards, and snakes. Antelopes, hippopotamuses, elephants, giraffes, wild dogs, leopards, and lions are diminishing in numbers. Common birds are quail, vultures, kites, and grey parrots. The kob, waterbuck, and reedbuck are found in the savanna region. A wildlife game preserve is near Jos where elephants, lions, and hippos can be observed from tourist cars.

Climate: Nigeria's tropical climate has warm temperatures and high humidity throughout the year, especially in the south. The average annual temperatures are about 80° F. (27° C) in the south and about 85° F. (29° C) in the north. The climate is hotter and drier in the north. Coastal areas receive about 150 in. (381 cm) of annual rainfall while the northern region receives less than 30 in. (78 cm) of precipitation. The wet season lasts from April to October, but is generally longer in the southern region. The hot and dry harmattan winds, blowing from the northeast, carry a reddish dust from the desert.

Greatest Distances: East-West: 800 mi. (1,287 km)
                                        North-South: 650 mi. (1,046 km)

Area: 356,669 sq. mi. (923,768 sq km)

ECONOMY AND INDUSTRY

Agriculture: Some 65 percent of the Nigerian workforce is engaged in agricultural activities, but less than 20 percent of the total land is under cultivation. The principal cash crops are cocoa, peanuts, oil palm, cotton, and rubber; food crops include rice, corn, taro, yams, cassava, sorghum, and millet. Livestock consists of goats, sheep, cattle, and poultry; cattle are raised primarily in the north. The country's coastal waters, lakes, rivers, and streams provide an abundance of fish and shrimp.

Mining: Nigeria is Africa's leading petroleum-producing country. Petroleum exports in the late 1980s provided more than 90 percent of the total export earnings. There are substantial deposits of natural gas and coal. Some tin, columbite, limestone, and iron ore also are mined. Oil refineries are located at Port Harcourt, Warri, and Kaduna.

Manufacturing: Manufacturing is primarily small scale and underdeveloped. The chief sectors of manufacturing are food processing, brewing, petroleum refining, iron and steel, motor vehicles, textiles, cigarettes, footwear, pharmaceutical, pulp and paper, and cement. There are some thirty commercial breweries in Nigeria producing excellent beer.

Transportation: Nigeria has a fairly extensive road network, almost half of which is paved. The major Nigerian cities are connected by roads and railroads. Many secondary roads are dirt roads. The inland waterways are about 5,400 mi. (8,500 km) long consisting of the Niger and the Benue Rivers and other smaller rivers and creeks. Lagos and Port Harcourt are the country's chief seaports. There are 14 airports with scheduled flights; both Lagos and Kano have international airports. The national airline is Nigerian Airways; it provides domestic and international service. Private airlines include Bellevue Airlines, Kabo Air, Zenith Air, Hold Trade Air, Trans-Sahel Airlines, and Okada Air.

Communication: Some 25 daily newspapers are published, mostly in English. The Nigerian press always has enjoyed a certain degree of freedom. Radio and television networks are under government control. Radio stations broadcast in more than a dozen languages. In the early 1990s there was one radio receiver per nine persons, one television set per 30 persons, and one telephone per 195 persons.

Trade: The chief imports are machinery and transport equipment, iron and steel products, textiles, paper products, chemicals, food items, and refined petroleum. The major import sources are Germany, the United Kingdom, the United States, and France. The chief export items are crude petroleum, cocoa beans, rubber, fertilizer, and cashew nuts. The major export destinations are the United States, Spain, Germany, The Netherlands, France, and Italy.

EVERYDAY LIFE

Health: Despite increasing medical facilities, malaria, tuberculosis, water-borne diseases, and meningitis are still prevalent, especially in the north. The introduction of new drugs has practically eliminated sleeping sickness. Providing primary health care is the responsibility of the basic health service scheme. Life expectancy at 54 years for males and 56 years for females is low. Infant mortality rate at 77 per 1,000 live births is high.

Education: Primary education begins at six years of age and lasts for six years. Secondary education begins at 12 years of age and lasts for a further 6 years, comprising two 3-year cycles. Education from 6 to 15 years is free and compulsory. In the early 1990s Nigeria had 31 universities and institutions of higher learning. The Ahmadu Bello University at Zaria is the largest. The International Institute of Tropical Agriculture is in Ibadan. There are Institutes of African Studies at the Universities of Ibadan and Ife. In the mid-1990s the literacy rate was about 51 percent.

Holidays:
   New Year's Day, January 1
   Id al-Fitr, March
   Easter, April
   Id al-Kabir, June
   Mouloud, August
   National Day, October 1
   Christmas, December 25

Id al-Fitr, Id al-Kabir, and Mouloud holidays are dependent on the Islamic lunar calendar and dates may vary every year; Easter is dependent on the Gregorian calendar.

Culture: Nigerian traditional art is among the most highly prized in the world. The oldest known African figure sculptures of terra-cotta were created in central Nigeria around 500 B.C. The National Museum in Lagos contains many valuable pieces of Nigerian art; it also has archaeological and ethnographic exhibits. Other cultural institutions in Lagos include the National Theater and the palace of the oba. The museum at Jos is the center of research into the prehistoric culture of Nigeria. Kano is the oldest major city in all of West Africa; it is the stronghold of Islamic learning with a famous central mosque. Oral Nigerian literature is rich in chants, folk stories, proverbs, and riddles. Traditional handicrafts include wood carvings, masks, baskets, decorative knives, painted gourds, colorful fabrics, and handmade jewelry.

Society: The mallamai are the Islamic scholars who often advise local officials and religious teachers. The Hausa Muslims blend a spirit cult, Bori, with their Islamic beliefs, to ward off evil. In Hausa society, women are considered belonging to a lower social scale just like butchers, hunters, or blacksmiths. In Islamic communities women are not allowed to attend some ceremonies and council meetings. In a village compound a Muslim man may have several wives. Each village has a chief or headman who settles disputes. Older children look after younger siblings; children are taught to show respect to their elders and parents. The local sultan of Sokoto is the religious leader of the Nigerian Muslims.

Music: Nigerian traditional musical instruments are made with local materials such as gourds, animal skins, shells, wood, and horns. Of all instruments, the drum is the most important. Pop music of Latin-American strains (conga and rumba), Western "swing" music, calypso from West Indies, "highlife" ballroom dance music, and modern American jazz, soul, and rock music are very popular. Juju music is the favorite of the younger generation.

Dress: In urban areas Nigerians wear Western-style clothing. Traditional Nigerian clothing, worn by both men and women in rural areas, consists of loose robes of white or brightly colored cotton or muslin fabrics. For headpieces, men wear small round caps while women often wear brightly colored scarves or turbans. Girls wear simple cotton dresses and boys loose shirts and shorts. Dressing up is very important to Nigerians in general. Several outfits are specially made with elaborate beadwork for special occasions like weddings. Traditional heavy robes are created by an ancient method called narrow strip weaving.

Housing: Rural houses are made of dried grass, mud, and wood and have thatch or corrugated metal roofs. Building material is dependent on the region of the country: dry areas have round clay houses with flat clay roofs, in the forest areas houses are rectangular with matted or tin roofs, and the coastal areas have bamboo houses. Groups of relatives live close by in a cluster of houses; several clusters make a village. Village compounds may be enclosed by walls of matting and sticks or of mud. Each compound has a garden of vegetables, tended by the women. Cities have modern apartment buildings.

Food: Nigerian food is very spicy. The chief items are corn, rice, beans, and yams; cassava roots, mangoes, and plantains also are popular. Peppers are used for seasoning. A porridgelike paste is made from the root of the cassava melon or from the seeds of millet grass. Lamb, chicken, or fish are eaten only occasionally. Devout Muslims do not eat pork or drink alcohol. Beer and palm wine are popular drinks.

Sports and Recreation: Soccer is the most popular sport. Traditional songs and dance are part of social gatherings. Musical instruments such as drums, xylophones, and various string and wind instruments are played during celebrations. Wedding celebrations last for days and are always accompanied by music, dancing, and festivities. The spectacular Durbar festival is held each year at the end of Ramadan in the city of Katsina.

Social Welfare: Benefits for sickness, retirement, and old age are operated by the national provident fund.

IMPORTANT DATES

500 B.C.-A.D. 200—The Nok civilization flourishes in central Nigeria

1000—The kingdom of Kanem adopts Islam as its religion

1352—Ibn Battuta, an Arab traveler, visits the western savanna region of present-day Nigeria

1400—The Portuguese are the first Europeans to arrive in Nigeria

1474—The first Portuguese traders reach Benin City

1500—Kano city-state becomes a center of trade and Muslim learning

1553—The first British expedition reaches Benin City

1500s-1600s—Portuguese missionaries introduce Christianity to Nigeria

1727—The Quakers make the first public protest in England against the practice of slave trading

1787—The Society for the Abolition of the Slave Trade is formed in England

1788—The African Association is formed in England to send expeditions to explore unknown territories of Africa

1802—The Danish government declares the slave trade illegal

1808—The British Parliament passes an act officially banning slave trade in British colonies; the United States forbids the import of any more slaves

1849—The British appoint a government representative, a consul of the Bights of Biafra and Benin; this marks the beginning of official British entry in Nigeria

1851—Great Britain seizes control of Lagos

1854—The discovery of quinine to treat malaria reduces health risks for Europeans in Africa

1885—The Berlin Conference divides Africa among European nations

1897—The British invade Benin City

1899—The British open the first nonreligious government school in Nigeria

1900—Nigeria becomes an official British colony

1908—Oil is discovered

1914—The northern and southern regions are joined into one unit by the British and called the Colony and Protectorate of Nigeria

1929—The "Women's Uprising" takes place in the Aba region near Port Harcourt

1939-45—During World War II, Nigerians fight for their colonial rulers

1946—The British divide Nigeria into three regions: north, west, and east

1947—A central Legislative Council is set up

1951—Nigerian male taxpayers are given the right to vote for their own representatives

1954—Nigeria becomes a self-governing federation; Lagos becomes a separate federal territory

1957—Sir Abubakar Tafawa Balewa becomes the federation's first prime minister

1959—Elections are held for the legislature

1960—Nigeria becomes an independent federal republic and a member of the Commonwealth of Nations; Parliamentary elections are held with all Nigerians voting, except women in the north where Islamic law forbids them voting

1961—The last British governor-general leaves Nigeria; Nigeria terminates the defense pact with the United Kingdom

1962—The National Library is founded in Lagos

1963—Nigeria becomes a republic with Dr. Benjamin Nnammdi Azikiwe as its president; the first census of an independent country is held

1966—Two separate army revolts take place in January and July; political parties and the legislature are suspended; a military government is established in Nigeria; Nigeria has five universities

1967—The independent republic of Biafra is declared in the eastern region; a civil war breaks out between Biafra and the rest of Nigeria

1968—The blockade of Biafra; a few countries recognize Biafra; the Kanji Dam Power Station is opened

1970—Biafran resistance collapses and Biafra ceases to exist; the civil war between Biafra and the rest of Nigeria ends

1971—Nigeria joins the Organization of Petroleum Exporting Countries (OPEC)

1972—Wole Soyinka leaves Nigeria to travel and teach in Africa, Europe, and the United States

1975—A bloodless coup takes place; the government takes over the state universities of Ife, Benin, Nsukka, and Zaria

1976—The government announces plans to transfer the capital from Lagos to Abuja; a new draft constitution is announced; the federal government sets up a universal primary education system; Wole Soyinka returns to Nigeria

1977—A constituent assembly is elected to draft a constitution

1978—State military governments are abolished; a ban on political parties is lifted; a new constitution is approved by the military government

1979—The nation's first civilian president in 13 years, Shehu Shagari, is elected; secondary education is made free; there are 13 universities in Nigeria

1980—The Nigerian population estimates are about 77 million

1982—Some 2 million non-Nigerian Africans are expelled from the country

1983—Nigeria suffers yet another military coup; a supreme military council is set up

1984—Sections of the constitution are suspended

1985—The supreme military council is renamed the armed forces ruling council; the Nigerian "Baby Eagles" win the Soccer World Cup for under-sixteens at the Commonwealth Games

1986—Nigeria restores full diplomatic relations with the United Kingdom; Wole Soyinka is awarded the Nobel Prize for literature

1987—Local elections are held in 300 electoral areas

1989—The ban on political parties is lifted; two new political parties are created; it is decided to move the capital from Lagos to Abuja

1990—Nigeria leads a multinational African peacekeeping force into Liberia to intervene in its civil war

1991—Nigeria sends troops to Sierra Leone; the capital is moved from Lagos to Abuja

1992—A population census takes place; general elections are held for Parliament

1993—Census estimates put the Nigerian population at 88.5 million, 20 million fewer than expected, and the results are disputed and challenged as gross underestimates; the first civilian presidential elections since 1983 are held, but a coup led by Major General Sani Abacha installed a military government rather than the election winner, M.K.O. Abiola; the United States, United Kingdom, and other European countries impose sanctions against Nigeria for suspending transition to civilian rule

1994—After his passport is confiscated and he is alerted he will be arrested, Wole Soyinka flees Nigeria; the market reforms initiated in 1986 are canceled by the military government; Nobel Prize–winning author Wole Soyinka discards his medal for "national merit," protesting the military government's treatment of M.K.O. Abiola; an eight-week-long oil strike almost cripples the oil industry

1995—Head of Nigeria's military government, Major General Sani Abacha, dismisses the civilian cabinet (known as the Federal Executive Council); government announces a series of economic reforms; ban is lifted from political activities; a new cabinet is selected; Mr. Saro-Wiwa, Africa's leading environmentalist, and eight other activists are hung on November 12 by the military government of Nigeria despite pleas from United States and European governments

IMPORTANT PEOPLE

Sani Abacha (1943-   ), military general, rose to power after the November 1993 coup

M.K.O. Abiola (1937-   ), winner of the 1993 presidential elections; he was arrested and imprisoned in June 1994 by Major General Sani Abacha

Chinua Achebe (1930-   ), novelist; has taught English at the Universities of Massachusetts and Connecticut; works include *Things Fall Apart, No Longer at Ease, Arrow of God, A Man of the People,* and *Anthills of the Savannah*

King Sunny Ade, leader of the African Beats juju music group

Chief Simeon Olaosebikan Adebo (1913-   ), diplomat; has held several United Nations posts

Major General Aguiyi-Ironsi (?-1966), an Igbo officer; led the military coup in 1966 and became head of state in January; assassinated in July of same year

Chief Yomi Akintolai (1939-   ), politician; member of the House of Representatives, 1979-83; member of the banned National Party of Nigeria (NPN)

Fela Anikulapo-Kuti (1938-), also known simply as Fela; developed Afro-Beat form of music, a combination of American Jazz and African music; his songs are highly critical of politicians; exiled to Ghana from 1978 to 1980; also sentenced to five years in prison in 1985, but was released in 1986 because of public protest

Dr. Benjamin Nnamdi Azikiwe (1904-), one of the leading West African Nationalists; first governor-general and president of independent Nigeria

Major General Ibrahim Badamasi Babangida (1941-), president of Nigeria 1985-93; introduced many reforms by cutting back government staff, putting more money in agriculture, and banning the import of foreign luxury items

Alhaji Sir Abubakar Tafawa Balewa (1912-66), the first prime minister of the federation; assassinated in the 1966 coup

Alhaji Sir Ahmadu Bello (1909-66), the hereditary leader of the Hausa-Fulani ruling class; became prime minister of the northern region in 1954

Major General Muhammad Buhari (1942-), leader of the bloodless coup in 1993 and then of the supreme military council; became head of state in 1983; ousted in 1985

Sokari Douglas Camp, Nigerian-born metal sculptor now living in London

J.P. Clark (1935-), writer, poet, playwright, educator

Samuel Ajayi Crowther (1809-92), a Yoruba missionary of the Church of England; he was made bishop of the Niger Territory in 1864

T. Obinkaram Echewa, writer; works include *I Saw the Sky Catch Fire*

Cyprian Ekwensi (1921-), novelist

Dr. Alex Ekwueme (1932-), architect; politician; vice president of the Federal Republic of Nigeria, 1979-83; detained by federal military government for almost 3 years and banned from political activity or holding political office

Taslim Olawale Elias (1914-), jurist; educator; professor of law and dean of Faculty of Law at University of Lagos, 1966-72; Chief Justice of Nigeria, 1972-75; judge, International Court of Justice, the Hague, since 1972

Buchi Emecheta, writer; named best black writer in Britain, 1978

Benedict Chuka Enwonwu (1921-94), Nigeria's leading artist and sculptor

Chief Ganiyu Oyesola Fawehinmi (1938-), lawyer; author; publisher; philanthropist; human rights activist; columnist for *Nigerian Tribune, Daily Sketch*, and *The Chronicle*; chairman, Free Education Association of Nigeria since 1975

Uthman dan Fodio (?-1819), founded the Fulani Empire at the beginning of the nineteenth century

General Yakubu Gowon (1934-), head of the federal military government 1966-75; formulated the post-civil war policy of reconciliation with the Igbos that resulted in the country's rapid recovery; ousted in a bloodless coup when he was attending an OAU meeting outside Nigeria

Aig Higo (1932-), poet

Chief Michael Christopher Onajirevbe Ibru (1932-), industrialist; outstanding international businessman

Chief Gabriel Osawaru Igbinedion (1934-), businessman; philanthropist

Louis Leakey (1903-72), British anthropologist; did pioneer work in human evolution

Dr. Afolabi Oladeinde Lucas (1941-), lawyer; insurance executive

Herbert Macaulay (1864-1946), considered the father of the Nigerian nationalism

Louis Nnamdi Mbanefo (1944-), lawyer; expert in maritime law

General Murtala Mohammed (?-1976), came to power in a military coup in 1975, but was assassinated the next year

Flora Nwapa, author of *Idu*, published in the 1960s

General Olusengun Obasanjo (1937-), head of the military government in the late 1970s; handed over power to a civilian government in 1979

Ebenezer Obey, leader of the juju music group Inter-Reformers Band

Chief Chukwuemeka Odumegwu Ojukwu (1933-), politician; head of state and commander in chief of Republic of Biafra, 1967-70; army general; member of banned National Party of Nigeria (NPN)

Gabriel Okara, writer; works include *The Voice*

Sonny Okosun, leader of an Afro-Beat band named Jungle Rock

Olowe of Ise, a master wood carver

Justice Charles Dadi Onyeama (1916-), lawyer; justice of the Supreme Court of Nigeria, 1964-67; judge, International Court of Justice, the Hague, 1967-76; chairman, University of Ife, 1976; part-time judge, World Bank Administrative Tribunal since 1982

Mungo Park (1771-1806), Scottish surgeon and explorer; one of the early explorers of the Niger River; commissioned by the British government in 1805 to explore the Niger River; wrote *Travels in the Interior of Africa* (1799)

Funmilayo Ransome-Kuti, activist for women's suffrage

Ken Saro-Wiwa (1941-95), writer; leading African environmentalist; Right Livelihood Award recipient 1994; Goldman Prize for the Environment 1995; Nobel Peace Prize nominee; he and eight other activists were hanged by the military government in 1995

Alhaji Shehu Shagari (1925-), first civilian elected president in 1979

Ernest Shonekan (1936-), acting president of Nigeria in 1993, just before the Sani Abacha coup

Dr. Tai Solarin (1922?-), politician; educator; social critic; author; member of banned National Party of Nigeria (NPN); publications include *Towards Nigeria's Moral Self-Government, Thinking With You, A Message for Young Nigerians,* and *To Mother with Love*

Wole Soyinka (1934-   ), novelist, poet, and playwright; awarded the 1986 Nobel Prize for literature, the first African to win this prize; works include *Aké: The Years of Childhood, Ìsarà: A Voyage Around "Essay," The Interpreters, The Man Died*

Dick Tiger (1929-71), sports figure; twice won world middleweight championship and world light-heavyweight championship once

Amos Tutuola (1920-   ), writer; writings are rich with Nigerian folktales; work includes *The Palm Wine Drinkard*

Dr. Joseph Wayas (1941-   ), politician; president of the Senate of the Federal Republic of Nigeria, 1979-83; political exile, 1984-87; in political detention, 1987-88

Compiled by Chandrika Kaul

INDEX

Page numbers that appear in boldface type indicate illustrations

About the Author

Dorothy B. Sutherland comes from Glasgow, Scotland, and has lived in London, Hamburg, New York, and Chicago. She has worked for many years in publishing and first became interested in Nigeria through working with books about it. She also has learned much about daily life there through many conversations with Nigerians in Chicago.

She is the author of *Scotland* and *Wales* in the Enchantment of the World series.